Innovative Octopuses, Half-Brained Birds,

and more animals with

Magnificent Minds

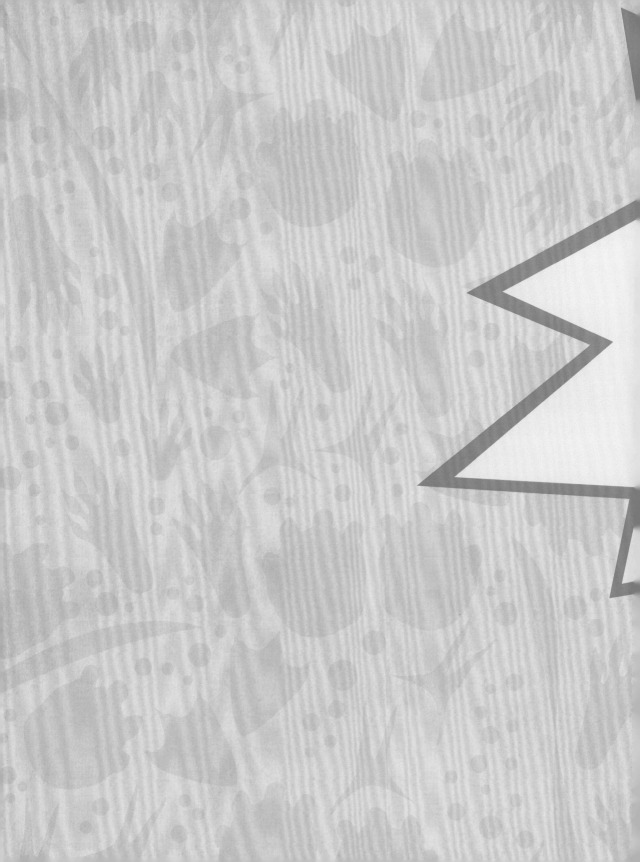

EXTRAORDINARY ANIMALS

Innovative Octopuses, Half-Brained Birds, and more animals with Magnificent Minds

Christina Couch

illustrations by **Daniel Duncan**

mit Kids Press

To Mom, Jason, and Lillian
CC

• • •

CONTENTS

INTRODUCTION

IN A CHICAGO AQUARIUM,

an octopus chips away at a block of ice, trying to get the frozen food inside. Her brain makes most of the decisions, but her sucker-covered arms make some choices all by themselves.

A bird nesting in Hawaii's high rocky cliffs catches a quick nap before heading out to hunt. Even as she's snoozing, half of her brain might be awake.

In a very special backyard in California, a squirrel decides where to stash food for the winter. She uses mind tricks to remember her hiding places.

And as you're reading this, a marvelous and mysterious organ inside your skull is working all day and all night to give you amazing abilities.

Large or small, smooth or wrinkly, brains of all shapes and sizes do extremely complicated work. Your brain weighs only about as much as a cantaloupe or a small pineapple, but crammed into that space is an electrically charged, lightning-fast biological machine with more processing power than the world's fastest supercomputer.

Your mind-blowing brain is the command center for your physical

functions, sensory systems, emotions, and thoughts, and even after centuries of studying it, scientists still have so much to learn and explore. The same is true for brains of other creatures, too. Brains vary a lot throughout the natural world, and their unique structures give animals abilities we just don't have.

In this book, you'll get to know six animals with incredible brain-powered talents and dive into the science behind these superpowers. You'll also learn about some of the things that happen between your own ears. On top of meeting a tortoise that seems to defy death, a parrot that helps humans mentally heal, and a whale that has its own wild way of communicating, you'll also learn about the people who study these creatures and the strategies they use to try to uncover the brain's many secrets. Plus, you'll get to put your own mind to the test with activities at the end of each chapter.

So put on your thinking cap and get ready to explore the animal kingdom's most extraordinary organ.

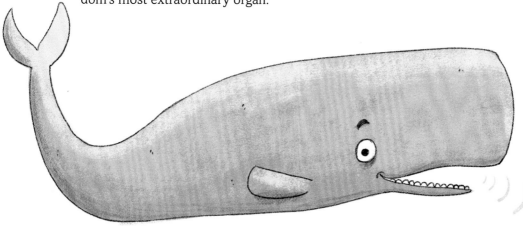

CHAPTER 1
INNOVATIVE OCTOPUSES

AT THE SHEDD AQUARIUM in Chicago, Illinois, the Oceans Gallery is Zoë Hagberg's favorite stop. Going behind the scenes, she walks up to a giant tank and lifts the lid to collect a water sample. Zoë cares for all kinds of animals at the aquarium, and testing the water in their tanks is part of her job. But in this tank, it isn't always easy: when Zoë dips a small bottle into the water, something red and slithery rushes up from the depths and tries to yank it out of her hand.

That sneaky, slippery snatcher is an arm that belongs to a giant Pacific octopus named Sawyer. For Sawyer, Zoë's visit means that it's playtime, and trying to grab the water-sample bottle is a great start. For the next thirty minutes, Zoë feeds Sawyer, gives her toys to play with (some with treats inside), and watches Sawyer carry her new playthings all around the tank. During the visit, Sawyer nibbles on raw shrimp frozen in blocks of ice and does the octopus version of licking everything she can, including Zoë. Each of Sawyer's eight arms has between 100 and 280 suckers that are packed with taste receptors. That means that whatever she touches, she tastes as well.

"Sometimes she touches my arms all the way up my bicep, but there have been a few people that she'll touch their skin and she'll recoil, like 'you did not taste good,'" Zoë says.

For Sawyer, all this playful exploring isn't just amusement—it's an important way to stay healthy. Just like people, octopuses thrive when they have new challenges. The ocean is full of places to explore, predators to escape, homes to build, and tasty food to find. But aquariums aren't nearly as full of new surprises. Without enough stimulation, octopuses can become stressed.

To keep their octo-pals engaged and happy, aquarium workers like Zoë come up with creative activities and play objects for them, just like you and your friends are always finding new things to do. But Sawyer's brain handles these challenges differently than yours does, in part because some decisions aren't made in her brain at all.

DID YOU KNOW?

Octopuses don't have tentacles. The eight appendages you see are actually arms—you can tell because they have suckers that run from the top all the way to the bottom. Tentacles, which are often longer and weaker than arms, have suckers only at the bottom or not at all. Just like octopuses, squid and cuttlefish have eight arms, but they also have two tentacles with clusters of suckers at the ends called clubs. They can shoot their tentacles out and grab prey with the clubs. Jellyfish, on the other hand, have tentacles without any suckers.

YOUR ELECTRICALLY CHARGED INFORMATION SPEEDWAY

Make two fists and put them together. That's roughly the size of your brain, and that small, fragile organ is in charge of *a lot* of stuff. It controls everything from your decisions, movements, thoughts, and feelings to your memories, senses, growth, and internal functions, like breathing and heart rate. That's so much for one brain to handle! But your brilliant brain is ready because it has an army of ultra-fast, super-organized, message-delivering marvels that work around the clock, year after year to coordinate all the incredible things your body can do. They're called **NEURONS**, or nerve cells, and they're a huge part of why all the different parts, organs, and cells in your body work together so well.

A neuron looks like a microscopic blob, with a long tail on one side and tiny, treelike branches sticking out on the other. Your brain has roughly 86 billion neurons—that's more than ten times the entire human population of earth—with many more in other parts of your body. Their biggest job is to zap information to nearby cells extremely quickly, faster than a race car driving at top speed. To you, information comes in lots of different forms—words, sounds, and pictures are just a few—but neurons send information using chemicals and tiny electrical pulses.

Here's how it works: let's say a friend playfully pokes you in the arm. That information needs to travel from your arm to your brain really fast so you can quickly decide what to do next. When your friend's finger comes in contact with your arm, sensory neurons in your skin react. Touch receptors pick up on the signal first. They pass that signal on to the neuron's thin branches, called **DENDRITES**, which transform it into an electrical pulse. This newly electrified signal heads into the neuron's cell body, and, if the signal is strong enough, it continues into the cell's tail, called the **AXON**, which might be super short, very long, or in between. When the signal gets to the end of the axon,

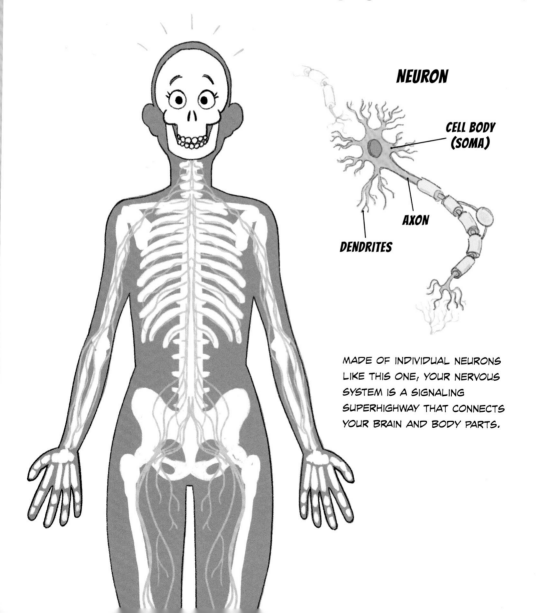

NEURON

CELL BODY (SOMA)

AXON

DENDRITES

MADE OF INDIVIDUAL NEURONS LIKE THIS ONE, YOUR NERVOUS SYSTEM IS A SIGNALING SUPERHIGHWAY THAT CONNECTS YOUR BRAIN AND BODY PARTS.

it has a unique way of getting to the next nerve cell. Neurons don't actually touch each other, so to pass the signal on, the neuron releases chemicals called **NEUROTRANSMITTERS** that carry the signal to nearby nerve cells.

This process happens fast—in a fraction of a second—and as the signal races from cell to cell, the message moves from neurons in your skin to your spinal cord, which acts like a superhighway straight to your brain. Long spinal nerves shoot signals from your limbs directly to your brain, so you can make the important decision of whether to poke your friend back.

And that's just one tiny example. Your body's amazing abilities require absolutely enormous amounts of cell communication and coordination—quadrillions of signals are sent and received every single second, both inside your brain and between your brain and the rest of your body. The giant network of neurons (and some other kinds of cells) that allows signals to quickly travel throughout your body and brain is called the **NERVOUS SYSTEM**.

And your brain? It's the nervous system headquarters, and it's always changing. As you grow, learn new things, and have new experiences, some neural pathways in your brain get stronger while others get weaker and disappear, making room for more learning. Brain networks can also change shape when people or animals get injured. Some people who have brain injuries can relearn skills they've lost, even if the parts of their brains that once ran those functions never fully recover.

People often think of the human brain, and the mighty network of neurons inside it, as the one and only decision-making organ in the body. The truth is a little different. For Sawyer, it's much different.

HOW MANY BRAINS DO YOU HAVE?

If you've ever had a gut feeling about something, there might be a scientific reason for that. Your digestive system is packed with neurons—somewhere between 200 million and 600 million of them—and they create a very chatty communication line between your gut and your brain.

Called the **GUT-BRAIN AXIS**, this communication line does a lot more than keep your digestion running. Neurons in the gut-brain axis send messages to regions of the brain that process emotions, which might be one reason why problems in our bellies can make us feel anxious or stressed, or why stressful situations can give us butterflies in our stomachs, stomachaches, or a sick feeling.

Studies show that bacteria and other microorganisms that live in our gut affect our moods and our ability to think clearly, though scientists are still learning about how that works. Researchers do know that changing the balance of gut bacteria in animals can make them more or less stressed and that some chemicals that are important for controlling your moods are made in your digestive tract, not your brain.

In fact, some scientists and doctors who make medicines to treat brain conditions look for inspiration in our gut—and also what comes out of it. Researchers at a few companies are currently studying human and animal poop, hoping to find clues they can use to make new treatments for conditions like depression and Parkinson's disease.

Some **NEUROSCIENTISTS** call the gut your "second brain" because of its special neurological connections. So, the next time you feel queasy before a big test or after seeing someone you have a crush on, know that it's just your other brain doing exactly what it's meant to do.

GUT-BRAIN AXIS: the communication pathways that run between your digestive tract and the rest of your nervous system

NEUROSCIENTIST: a scientist who studies the brain, spinal cord, and network of cells that carry messages within the brain and between the brain and other parts of the body

A BODY WITH A MIND OF ITS OWN?

Just like you, octopuses are creative problem-solvers. In the wild, they defend themselves with just about anything they can find, from coconut shells to stingers they rip from other marine animals. They're champions of deception and can escape predators by vanishing in bursts of ink, by cutting off their own arms and hurling them as distractions, or by changing their skin's color and texture to blend into their surroundings or to mimic an even scarier predator.

CAN YOU SPOT THE SNEAKY OCTOPUS HERE? TURN THIS BOOK UPSIDE DOWN FOR A CLUE! HINT: LOOK NEAR THE MIDDLE OF THE PHOTO.

In labs and aquariums, octopuses beat mazes and puzzles, ace simple memory tests, and sometimes even outwit the people who study and care for them. These eight-armed escape artists are famous for breaking out of their tanks and causing total mayhem. Rogue octos have slid across aquarium floors to dine on fish in other tanks and squeezed into drainpipes and flushed themselves into the ocean. They've even taken water valves apart and accidentally flooded entire buildings.

Octopuses like Sawyer use their brains to do all of these things, but not exactly the way a human would, says Jennifer Mather, a

OCTOPUSES ARE EIGHT-ARMED ESCAPE ARTISTS.

ALIENS AMONG US

People and octopuses both have incredible problem-solving skills. And the fact that our brains approach and process problems so differently might be important beyond this planet.

We humans have some key things in common with our octo-friends—we're both physically weak compared to other animals, are vulnerable to many types of predators, and live in tough environments. For many people, threats like hungry beasts are no longer daily problems, but millions of years ago, they were matters of life and death for almost everyone.

Back then, the humans who figured out new ways to find food, make shelter, and avoid or outsmart predators were more likely to survive and have babies. Humans taught each other survival skills they had learned, but they also passed down biological traits that helped our ancestors come up with creative ways of solving problems. Over time, these traits were passed down more and more until, eventually, we all had them. This process of gradual change to brains and bodies that happens when organisms pass down traits is called **EVOLUTION**.

EVOLUTION: the process by which species biologically change over generations

Octopuses evolved sharp problem-solving skills, too, but in a totally separate way from humans. And that's interesting to people who study life on Earth and to **ASTROBIOLOGISTS** like Dominic Sivitilli. Astrobiologists study things like how we might detect life beyond Earth, what kinds of organisms could survive in different outer-space environments, and how those life-forms might change over time. Octopuses, and their unique networks of neurons, show how intelligence can evolve in bodies that are very different from our own.

ASTROBIOLOGIST: a scientist who studies how life might develop in other places in the universe

"Alien intelligence is probably not going to look human," Dominic says. Aliens "might have centralized brains, but they might not. An octopus is fundamentally built differently from us. Its skin is different. Its brain and sensory organs are different, but just like us, they're very intelligent. They show us a new path to intelligence."

Dominic says that most astrobiologists don't study octopuses—instead, they're much more likely to focus on microscopic organisms that live in our planet's most extreme environments, like in underwater volcanoes where temperatures are much, much hotter than boiling water or in nuclear materials where radiation levels might be more than five hundred times higher than the amount that a person can stand. These habitats are more similar to environments on other planets. But looking at animals like octopuses that were living on Earth long before the dinosaurs can give clues about how life starts, changes, and ends, here and maybe even beyond.

DUMBO OCTOPUSES LIKE THIS ONE LIVE DEEP DOWN IN THE OCEAN—
UP TO 13,000 FEET (NEARLY 4,000 METERS) BENEATH THE SURFACE.

scientist at the University of Lethbridge in Canada who studies how octopuses think and perceive the world. Sawyer's brain looks different from yours: it's much smaller and it's shaped like a donut. Her esophagus, which carries food from her mouth to her stomach, runs right through the middle. (In fact, unlike lots of other sea creatures, Sawyer has to break down her meal some before she swallows it. Otherwise, a mouthful of spiny or sharp foods could tear her esophagus and cause brain damage!)

Octopuses have neurons, too—about five hundred million, which is tiny compared to the number you have—but their neurons aren't concentrated as much in the brain region like yours are. Sawyer has big clusters of neurons along her arms, and these can sometimes work together to do things without communicating with her brain.

"The brain makes all the big decisions," Jennifer explains, "but it leaves an awful lot of the details of what to do to the arms."

For example, she adds, if an octopus decides to walk—yep, they can walk along the ocean floor, usually using their four back arms—neurons in the arms, not the brain, might coordinate how to carry out that action.

Your body also reacts sometimes without input from your brain. Let's say you touch something *really* hot. That message doesn't have time to travel all the way to your brain and back before you get burned. So neurons in your fingers shoot that information to the neurons in your spinal cord, which tell your fingers, "Hey! Get out of there fast!" These split-second, automatic reactions are called **REFLEXES**, and octopuses take them to the next level. Detach an octo arm, for instance, and the arm can still move—no brain required.

Because octopus arms are more indepen-dent from the brain than our arms and legs,

REFLEX: an involuntary action that does not require conscious thought

some might think that each octopus arm has its own mini-brain. But Jennifer says that's not right. "There's only one brain," she says, "and that controls all the big stuff."

Scientists have a lot of questions about exactly when octopus arms communicate with the brain and when they don't. Scientists like Jennifer who study octopuses are still figuring out how these arms coordinate with each other—and how they help octopuses find new solutions to problems.

Back in Chicago, Sawyer and Zoë aren't worried about those questions—they're too busy having fun. When playtime is over, Zoë's shirt is soaked from wet octopus touches and Sawyer is carrying a toy from Zoë back to her den. With Sawyer fed, Zoë carefully shuts the lid to the tank and double-checks that it's properly closed and locked. Sawyer hasn't escaped before, but Zoë isn't taking any chances.

A GIANT PACIFIC OCTOPUS AT THE SHEDD AQUARIUM GETS A TOY.

LEFT, RIGHT, AND EVERYTHING IN BETWEEN

Have you ever heard a person described as being either left-brained or right-brained? Left-brained people are supposedly more logical and analytical, the ones who are naturally good at math, science, and organizational thinking. So-called right-brainers, on the other hand, tend to be more artistic and creative and excel in visual thinking, imaginative projects, music, and literature.

Both phrases come from neuroscience: your brain really does have left and right halves, and each handles different duties. But after that, the left-versus-right-brain theory falls short. Lots of research shows that big mental tasks, like solving math problems or making art, require both brain hemispheres, and subjects that we often think of as "logical" involve heaps of creative thinking. But let's hear from some people who know this firsthand. For these scientists, the analytical work they do in the lab is made better by the creative things they do outside it.

OUTSIDE OF THE LAB, RUBY IBARRA IS A RAPPER, DIRECTOR, AND SPOKEN WORD ARTIST.

RHYMES AND ENZYMES

By day, Ruby Ibarra is a scientist near San Francisco, California, who helps develop medical testing kits that are used by labs around the world. At night, she grabs the mic. Outside of her scientific work, Ruby is a rapper and poet who's appeared in magazines, commercials, and on billboards. For her, one world improves the other.

"When we're doing new projects or experiments in the lab, music has shown me that it's okay to think outside of the box," she says. "That's helped me stop feeling stuck when I'm not getting the lab results I want."

The reverse is also true, she adds. "When it comes to writing my lyrics or writing poetry, I'm very methodical about it," she says. "Ultimately, it's helped me to be a better artist."

BATTLES AND BUGS

Friends call her Anahí. Roller derby fans call her Victoria Amazonica—a name inspired by one of her favorite plants. At the University of Maryland in College Park, Anahí Espíndola studies bugs that polli-

RUBY HAS TOURED ACROSS THE UNITED STATES AND THE PHILIPPINES.

nate, and she says that the lessons she learned from six years of whipping around the track on roller skates help her in the lab today.

ANAHÍ ESPÍNDOLA IS A FORCE ON WHEELS AND IN THE LAB.

Anahí recently retired from roller derby, but she says that her derby skills help her run her lab like a team. Scientists often work with researchers who study completely different things than they do, and communicating complex concepts can be challenging. But athletes are trained to be all-star communicators, and roller derby is no exception. "It goes very fast and you have to communicate in a very clear way," Anahí says. "It's really important to know when you're not being understood and how you can improve."

In her lab, Anahí leads many of the same team-building exercises she did in her derby days, and they've helped scientists work together to create new research strategies and lend a hand when someone's stuck on a problem.

FISH AND FLIPS

If Elizabeth Sibert isn't examining an ancient fish with a microscope, she's probably hanging from the ceiling. At the Woods Hole Oceanographic Institution in Massachusetts, Elizabeth studies fossilized fish and sharks and traces how these creatures transformed over millions of years. Outside of the lab, she's a high-flying circus performer who swings, flips, and does stunts on long fabric suspended high in the air, and she teaches others to do the same. "As long as my feet aren't touching the ground, I'm a really happy person," she says.

Fish teeth and circus acts may not appear to go together, but Elizabeth says that her laboratory and performing work both require creative thinking and an ability to teach tough concepts in many different ways. Studying fossils is "like getting in a time machine, but it's a little broken and can only give us tiny snippets of the past. We have to be able to take those snippets and build a story to figure out what they're telling us about a world that we can't see," she says. "Being able to think creatively and explain things in many different ways is a very useful skill for that."

ELIZABETH SIBERT THINKS CREATIVELY ON THE GROUND AND IN THE AIR.

ACTIVITY
RAPID RESPONSES

How quickly do messages travel to your brain and back? And is it the same for your friends? In this activity, you'll put your nervous system to the test.

YOU'LL NEED:
- a partner (this could be a parent, relative, or friend you can do the activity with)
- a ruler
- a table or desk
- paper
- a writing utensil

1. Have your partner rest their arm on the table with one hand sticking out over the edge.

2. Hold the ruler in a straight, vertical line, with the lowest number at the bottom and the highest one at the top. Position the ruler just above, but not touching, the tips of your partner's fingers, and turn it so that the number side is facing the inside of your partner's thumb. (Stay away from the inside of their hand.)

3. Tell your partner to open their hand so that they're ready to catch the ruler with the tips of their thumb and index finger.

4. Tell them that you're going to let go of the ruler—you won't tell them when—and that they should catch it as quickly as they can.

5. When you're ready, let go of the ruler and when they catch it, write down the centimeter or inch mark that's closest to the middle of their thumb.

6. Repeat the whole challenge at least three times (or more if you're having fun). Did your partner's measurements stay the same every time, or did they react faster with practice?

7. Now switch roles and test your reaction time. Repeat steps 1–6, then look for patterns in your results. Who had the fastest time in a single trial? Who was the fastest across all of the trials? Did one of you improve their reaction time more than the other?

BONUS

As you get more practice with this activity, you'll likely have faster reaction times. But what happens if you change the rules of this activity just a little? If you switch hands, and your partner does the same when it's their turn to catch the ruler, does your reaction time change? What happens if you close your eyes and your partner says a code word just before they drop the ruler? Scientists frequently do many different versions of the same experiment. Try coming up with your own rules and see what happens.

CHAPTER 2
PANIC-BUSTING PARROTS

AT THIS RESCUE CENTER, THE PEOPLE HEAL THE BIRDS AND THE BIRDS HEAL THE PEOPLE.

OUTSIDE OF LOS ANGELES, California, a bright blue-and-green parrot named Jester calmly looks around and stretches out his wings. Jester wasn't always this relaxed, but over time, he's changed, just a little each day. So has a man who takes care of him.

Jester lives at Serenity Park Sanctuary, a special home for birds that have been abandoned, neglected, or abused. About thirty-five birds live at the sanctuary, and they've all been through terrible things—some were left completely alone and locked in tiny cages; others were starved or were hurt in ways that prevent them from ever flying again. Jester was mistreated for a long time and came to Serenity Park needing to heal.

"The animals here are scared, fearful. They don't know how to trust," says Stan McDonald, a Serenity Park worker who cares for Jester. "That was the same way I was."

Stan has also had extremely difficult, sometimes terrifying, experiences that still affect his mind and body years after they happened. Jester is an important part of how Stan's brain is healing. At Serenity Park, people who have been through **TRAUMA** work with birds that have, too. They help each other get better, but it's not easy.

TRAUMA: a physical and emotional response to a deeply stressful or frightening event

THALAMUS: *a part of the brain that's important for sensory processing, movement, attention, consciousness, language, and memory functions*

FEAR FACTORS

Your body has an entire system that helps you deal with fear and stress, says Antonia Seligowski, a neuroscientist who studies fear and trauma at McLean Hospital in Boston, Massachusetts. When you first perceive danger, your eyes or ears send that information to the **THALAMUS**, which is shaped like an egg and located right in the middle of your brain. The thalamus has many jobs—it's involved in sleeping and wakefulness, attention, and memory, and it also acts kind of like a train station for your senses. Signals from your sight, sound, taste, and touch receptors all pass through the thalamus, then get routed wherever they need to go next. (Smell is the exception. Odor receptors don't send signals through the thalamus and scientists are still researching why.)

When you're facing a fearful situation, that next stop is your **AMYGDALA**—a tiny, almond-shaped cluster of cells located close to the thalamus. Scientists are still learning about exactly how the amygdala works and all of the different things it does—that's true for most other parts of the brain, too—but they do know that amygdala cells are important for processing many different emotions. When you're scared, they help translate information from your senses into chemical messages that alert your body: Pay attention! Trouble is ahead!

AMYGDALA: *a part of the brain that helps process emotions and stress*

Now it's time to get the rest of your body ready to take action. To do that, your amygdala passes those distress signals to two different places. One is the **HIPPOCAMPUS**—a curvy part of the brain that's involved in memory. (Remembering scary experiences can help you avoid danger in the future.)

HIPPOCAMPUS: *a part of the brain that plays a major role in learning and memory*

MIND MONSTERS

If you want to know how the hippocampus got its name, look to the deep blue sea. In Greek, *hippos* means horse, and *kampos* means sea monster or sea animal. In Greek mythology, the hippocamps were full-size underwater horses with fish tails. Some people believed that these creatures pulled chariots for Poseidon, the god of the oceans and of horses.

In the 1500s, when an Italian scientist named Julius Caesar Arantius was dissecting human brains and describing what was inside, he noticed a peculiar-looking part deep within the brain. It had a thick, rounded end that looked a little like a head and a thinner tail that curled inward, almost like a seahorse's. He knew exactly what to call it. Real seahorses—the kind you've probably seen—have the scientific name *Hippocampus*, likely because of their horse-like features and curled tails.

The hippocampus isn't the only thing inside your head that's named after an animal. A bumpy bone that's part of your skull, just above the spot between your two eyebrows, is called the crista galli, which translates to rooster's comb or crest in Latin.

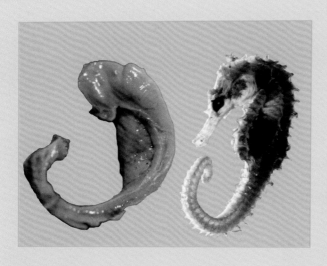

IS THERE A SEA CREATURE IN YOUR BRAIN? HERE'S THE ONE IN YOUR HEAD COMPARED TO THE ONE IN THE OCEAN.

HYPOTHALAMUS: *a part of the brain that helps control your body's response to stress*

The amygdala also sends distress signals to a cone-shaped part of your brain called the **HYPOTHALAMUS**, which operates almost like a megaphone to the rest of your body. Your hypothalamus helps with memories, but it also serves as a communication hub between your brain and millions and millions of cells, from your head all the way down to your toes. The hypothalamus sends out a tsunami of chemical messages announcing that it's go time. Your body leaps into action.

Nerve cells in nearly all of your organs get to work, often without you even noticing. Your breathing rate increases and energy levels shoot up. Your muscles tense, ready to help you move in fractions of a second. Your vision and hearing get sharper, and your body stops doing things that might slow you down, like producing saliva and digesting food. "All of that is helping you be stronger and more capable of running away or fighting," Antonia says. Together, all of the nerve cells that respond to stress are called the **SYMPATHETIC NERVOUS SYSTEM**.

But being this hyperalert takes *a lot* of energy. Luckily, your body also has ways to calm down. When the threat is gone, your hypothalamus sends new chemical messages that tell your body: *Relax! The coast is clear!* These messages go to the cells in your **PARASYMPATHETIC NERVOUS SYSTEM**, which scientists sometimes call your "rest and digest system." Your breathing and heart rate slow down; pupils, muscles, and digestion return to normal; and energy levels drop. You might even need sleep—being scared is exhausting.

SYMPATHETIC NERVOUS SYSTEM: *a network of nerves that operate your body's response to fear and stress*

PARASYMPATHETIC NERVOUS SYSTEM: *a network of nerves that bring your body back to a calm state after experiencing fear or stress*

FEAR AFFECTS YOU FROM HEAD TO TOE. HERE ARE SOME WAYS THAT YOUR BODY RESPONDS.

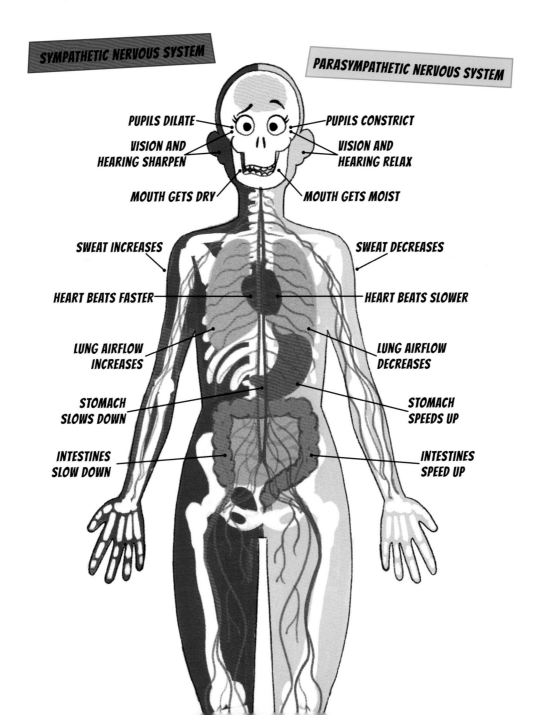

SYMPATHETIC NERVOUS SYSTEM

PARASYMPATHETIC NERVOUS SYSTEM

PUPILS DILATE

PUPILS CONSTRICT

VISION AND HEARING SHARPEN

VISION AND HEARING RELAX

MOUTH GETS DRY

MOUTH GETS MOIST

SWEAT INCREASES

SWEAT DECREASES

HEART BEATS FASTER

HEART BEATS SLOWER

LUNG AIRFLOW INCREASES

LUNG AIRFLOW DECREASES

STOMACH SLOWS DOWN

STOMACH SPEEDS UP

INTESTINES SLOW DOWN

INTESTINES SPEED UP

Fear isn't bad, Antonia adds. It helps protect you. But being in truly terrifying situations can overpower the body's ability to cope and make people feel afraid even when danger isn't there anymore. Seeing or experiencing life-threatening events can change how the brain perceives and processes danger. For some people, that can mean experiencing events from long ago as if they're happening right now.

GHOSTS FROM THE PAST

Before coming to Serenity Park, Stan McDonald served in the US Navy. After going through a tough childhood, where he experienced abuse and neglect, he joined the military to try to make his life more stable. It did. The days were structured. He made friends and felt secure. Then, in the 1990s, the United States sent almost seven hundred thousand troops to the Middle East to fight in the Persian Gulf War. Stan was one of them. He was sent into combat zones twice. He saw lots of violence. Some of his friends died. He stayed alert, knowing that something devastating could happen at any moment.

That feeling wouldn't go away, even after he left the combat zone. When Stan left the military and returned home, he had a hard time settling back in. He was angry much of the time and had trouble sleeping and concentrating. He couldn't trust people, even those he loved most. Bad memories haunted his thoughts and dreams, and when certain things reminded him of those experiences, it was almost as if his brain time-traveled back to the instant when they happened. Those moments weren't the same as memories—Stan felt like he was really back there, the fear rushing through him.

Stan started using alcohol to push down the bad feelings. Soon, it became an addiction. In 2007, he went to a treatment center for veterans called New Directions. That's where Stan found a name for his condition—**POST-TRAUMATIC STRESS DISORDER**, or PTSD for short. He also found Lorin Lindner, a mental health doctor and the clinical director of New Directions

who had also started a parrot sanctuary near the treatment facility. Lorin's team hired veterans—many from New Directions—to care for sick, injured, and abused birds.

POST-TRAUMATIC STRESS DISORDER (PTSD):
A condition that results in people experiencing lasting mental and emotional stress following a traumatic event. Nightmares, concentration and memory problems, and feelings of anger, detachment, or reliving the event are common symptoms.

DR. LORIN LINDNER
AND SAMMY THE BIRD

When Stan first entered New Directions, he couldn't trust or talk to therapists: "I was not going to open up to them," he says. But when he started volunteering with the Serenity Park parrots later that year, something shifted. Suddenly, he was face-to-face with beautiful, hurt animals that needed help—birds that had no reason to trust people but, with enough time and kindness, eventually did.

Stan saw these birds change in just a few months. Their injuries healed. Underfed parrots became plump and energetic again. Birds that once screeched or attacked him when he cleaned out their enclosures steadily inched closer and stayed calmer as the weeks passed. And the more they trusted Stan, the more he trusted them. He started talking to the birds and eventually began telling them about his experiences.

STAN GETS PERSONAL WITH A SERENITY PARK PARROT.

"By talking to the animals, I was learning to get it out, let it go, you know, learning how to live," he says. "Eventually, I was able to talk to the doctors because the animals taught me how to trust."

Seven years later, when Jester arrived at Serenity Park, Stan was a lot healthier. He wasn't as angry anymore or overwhelmed by bad memories.

JESTER (LEFT) AND TANGO SHARE A SPACE AT SERENITY PARK SANCTUARY.

"THE ANIMALS TAUGHT ME HOW TO TRUST."

He had stopped drinking alcohol and was more comfortable talking about his feelings. Though his PTSD symptoms might not ever fully go away, they were much more manageable thanks to therapy. He was even helping Lorin Lindner run another rescue center for wolves and similar species. Stan was in a better place, and he was prepared to take care of a bird who wasn't.

MAKING THE CASE

Scientists have a lot of questions about why, and how much, building animal bonds can improve our mental health. Anxious people who pet a friendly animal, even for just a few minutes, feel calmer afterward. When therapy programs incorporate animals, patients often report feeling more relaxed, happier, and better able to communicate with their therapists. Animals might also improve our physical health, too— some research shows that people who regularly interact with pets or therapy animals have lower heart rates, lower risk of heart disease, and less physical pain.

But some scientists say that we need more large-scale, well-designed studies in this field to really know if animals cause positive long-term changes. Most studies on animal therapy are small and don't include a huge number of participants, which leaves researchers unsure of how much the results of these studies apply to everyone. Some studies also aren't designed in ways that let researchers directly compare patients who interacted with animals to those who didn't. Though most studies have found that therapy with animals has positive health benefits, many don't examine those effects over long periods of time, and a few studies didn't find any effects at all.

Figuring out how to sort through limited and conflicting evidence is part of a scientist's job. Researchers often look at lots of studies and debate what truths can be drawn and how they can design new experiments to get clearer results.

COMING IN HOT

Jester came ready to fight. Jester is part military macaw and part blue-and-gold macaw—two species that are known for their bright, rainbow-colored feathers. But when he got to Serenity Park, Jester had patches of bald, scarred skin showing. He was thin from not having the right food, and his tail was curled under his body, which happens when long-tailed birds are kept in cages that are too small. He bit anything he could, including himself.

The Serenity Park team doesn't have very much information about Jester's life before he got to the rescue center, but they know that he was mistreated, didn't have the food or space he needed, and didn't have a flock of other birds like wild parrots do. When Jester arrived at the sanctuary in 2015, "he automatically went on the attack," Stan says.

But just like Stan, Jester changed with time and care. After moving to Serenity Park, Jester received good nutrition, space to stretch out, and closeness to other birds. He grew stronger and healthier, and Stan started visiting every day. He would stand outside Jester's wide enclosure. The bird would screech and try to attack, but Stan stayed relaxed and still, talking to Jester in a soothing voice. "Slowly, he realized nothing was happening," he says. "I wasn't trying to fight back."

After a few months, Jester started inching closer to the wire fence near Stan, then eventually let him put his finger through the wire. Six months after coming to Serenity Park, Jester let Stan pet his beak. "That was basically the turning point right there," he says.

Today, Jester is a much calmer, well-fed bird. His skin has healed and some of his feathers have grown back in, though he still has bald patches.

FEAR IN THE WILD

There isn't very much neuroscience research that explores how birds experience fear or long-term mistreatment. But animals who go through events that cause trauma in humans sometimes show similar signs of PTSD. In combat zones, for example, military dogs that are trained to help soldiers by sniffing out enemies or explosives experience the same gunfire, bombings, and violence that soldiers do. Just like traumatized people, some military dogs become panicky and respond aggressively. Some stop being able to do their jobs—among the 650 service dogs the United States deployed to Iraq and Afghanistan, 5 to 10 percent showed signs of canine PTSD.

Liana Zanette, an **ECOLOGIST** at Western University in Ontario, Canada, studies how fear affects wild animals. She says that, just like in humans, fear can have long-lasting effects. Many of Liana's studies involve playing sound recordings of predators for days or even months in wild settings. She's found that when animals such as song sparrows, badgers, and raccoons heard sounds of their predators, they spent more time watching for danger and less time eating during that period.

These fear-inspired behaviors can have huge impacts. In one study, for example, song sparrows that heard predator sounds over three breeding seasons had fewer and less-healthy babies compared to sparrows that didn't hear those sounds. Those lower birth and survival rates make a big difference over time—Liana's team estimated that the population of sparrows in the frightened group would drop by more than half in the next few years.

Liana has also found some brain similarities between people and birds that experience fear. Wild black-capped chickadee birds that heard predator calls for two days had very active amygdalae and hippocampi a week later—researchers have seen similar patterns in people with PTSD. Liana says that her work, and research by other scientists on animals in labs, shows that PTSD probably isn't unique to people: "You're not the same person or the same animal that you were before experiencing it."

ECOLOGIST: a scientist who studies how living things interact with their environment

When Stan visits, Jester freely allows him to come into the enclosure. Stan is no longer overwhelmed by the trauma he experienced, and Jester seems less stressed, too. Scientists are studying how to help humans or animals heal from trauma; Stan is happy to be living proof that they can. And Jester appears to be on his way, too.

STAN SAYS THAT OPENING UP TO THE SERENITY PARK PARROTS HELPED HIM OPEN UP TO PEOPLE.

CREATURE COMFORTS

Animals are known for helping people through tough times and new challenges. Some, like pets or the Serenity Park parrots, bring joy just by living their daily lives. Others are trained as therapy animals and work in places like nursing homes, schools, and summer camps.

Therapy animals might be trained to help people who have gone through traumatic events, but they can also work in places where people experience everyday stress. Here are a few of our favorite anxiety-easing animals.

ALEX THE AIRPORT BUNNY

At the San Francisco International Airport in California, nervous flyers have an entire squad of four-legged cheerleaders that are there to make traveling a little more fun. The Wag Brigade is a group of trained ther-

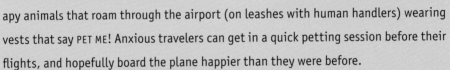

apy animals that roam through the airport (on leashes with human handlers) wearing vests that say PET ME! Anxious travelers can get in a quick petting session before their flights, and hopefully board the plane happier than they were before.

Alex is a Flemish giant rabbit—a species known for being tame and friendly with people—and the only bunny member of the Wag Brigade, which also includes dogs plus one pig, named LiLou. Since Alex started making rounds in the airport, he's proven that he's just as calm, capable, and cuddly as the rest of the team.

ROSIE THE PICK-ME-UP PIG

For those living at the Czorny Alzheimer Centre in Surrey, Canada, days are a little cheerier when a pig comes to say hi. The center is home to many people who have health conditions that affect their thinking and memories, but their most famous resident is Rosie the therapy pig, who happily accepts pats and warm cuddles from anyone who needs to take their mind off of medical stuff. Rosie visits residents and entertains them with tricks, like shaking a hoof or spinning in a circle, and she also welcomes guests herself. During certain hours, anyone living at, visiting, or working in the center can stop by Rosie's indoor barn for a quick mood boost.

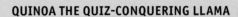

QUINOA THE QUIZ-CONQUERING LLAMA

If you've ever felt nervous before a big test, you know how stressful school can be. At the University of California, Berkeley, college students have a unique strategy for dialing down their jitters just before final exams: hanging out with some llamas. Every year, the campus holds an event called Llamapalooza, where students give local therapy llamas snuggles and snacks while getting a much-needed study break. Quinoa, from the nearby Llamas of Circle Home ranch, is a popular star at Llamapalooza.

LEGEND THE BOOK BUDDY

Reading aloud makes some people nervous. Legend is there to help. This golden retriever visits public libraries in Plymouth, Massachusetts, and listens to kids practice their reading skills in a private, quiet environment. Readers get a chance to speak at their own pace and practice without judgment while Legend gets plenty of pets and

an afternoon of good stories. Libraries and schools throughout North America and beyond host Read to a Dog programs. There might be one near you.

ACTIVITY
MEDITATION MIND-BENDER

Meditation is a practice many people use to calm their nervous systems and help themselves feel more relaxed. Studies show that even a few minutes of meditation every day can sharpen your mental focus, help you feel less anxious, and provide a strategy you can use to clear your head when things get stressful. Historians think meditation originated in India and that people have been meditating for thousands of years. This beginner meditation exercise will give you a chance to try it for yourself.

YOU'LL NEED:

- a bed or comfy spot on the floor

Since you'll have your eyes closed, read the instructions all the way through before you try it, or have a partner read them out loud to you.

1. Lie on your back, place your hands on your belly, and close your eyes.

2. First, you'll need to calm down and get settled into the activity. To do that, take two or three deep, steady breaths in and out while you're lying down. Pay attention to your chest rising and falling.

3. Now that you're settled in, keep your breathing steady and your hands resting on your belly. Focus your thoughts on your toes and only on your toes. What do your toes feel right now? Maybe you feel socks if you're wearing them, or a cool breeze blowing by. Do they feel totally relaxed? Or jittery? Try to feel each part of your toes—from the very tip-top all the way to the bottom—but don't try to change the way they feel.

4. After thinking about your toes for about three or four breaths in and out, shift your focus to the rest of your feet, minus your toes, and repeat step 3. For a few breaths, pay attention to how your heels, arches, and the tops of your feet feel. Can you feel them touching the bed or the floor? Are they leaning to one side or the other? Are they getting more relaxed? Don't think about any other part of your body, just your feet.

5. Focus like this on the rest of your body, one part at a time from the bottom up. Spend a few breaths focusing on your ankles, then your lower legs, then your upper legs, all the way up to your torso, arms, and head. If your mind wanders, that's okay—just stay still, let it pass, and refocus when you can.

6. When you're done, take a few more breaths and focus on your whole body. Does it feel different now than it did before you started? Now take note of your mental state. Does your mind feel calmer? Sleepier? Or does it feel more awake?

BONUS

Try doing this exercise before you have to do something that makes you nervous. Does clearing your mind beforehand affect how you approach that uncomfortable task?

CHAPTER 3
SAVVY SQUIRRELS

GREEN·EAR·22·1120 has found the squirrel equivalent of gold. In a backyard in Novato, California, this young eastern gray squirrel, who we'll just call Green, picks up a nut from a tray, shakes it around a few times, and turns it over in her tiny paws. It's autumn now, and nuts like these will be crucial for surviving the shorter, colder days of winter. But this nut-filled back-yard is unlike any other: as Green decides what to do with her prize, scientists are quietly watching how she stores the food she finds.

Green is a student in Squirrel School, a program run by biologist Lucia Jacobs at the University of California, Berkeley. Lucia has studied squirrels for about forty years, and she's fascinated by how these creatures map and navi-gate their surroundings, especially when it comes to food. Like some birds and other rodents, many squirrel species are **SCATTER-HOARDERS**: they stockpile food by storing bits in many different places. Squirrels like Green bury lots of food—usually between three thousand

SCATTER-HOARDER: an animal that stores food by hiding it in many different places and five thousand seeds and nuts each year—"and they're doing it really fast," Lucia adds, usually in roughly six weeks.

Then comes the tough part—remembering where their supplies are during the months ahead. Instead of making treasure maps as humans do, squirrels use memory strategies and their brain biology to remember the different locations where they buried their treats. To learn more about this ability and others, Lucia partnered with an animal hospital and education organization called WildCare, which treats orphaned and injured wildlife and then releases them back into nature. Together, they launched Squirrel School—a place where animals like Green can safely ease back into their natural habitats before being fully released into nature, and where scientists can observe their remarkable brains in action along the way.

MAKING MEMORIES

The ability to store and retrieve information is a crucial survival skill for humans and for lots of other animals. Memories help us get through daily life and hold valuable information about who we are, what we've experienced, and what we want for the future. Your brain is a magnificent memory-making marvel that traps everything from math formulas to which drawer holds your socks to the happiest feeling you've ever felt, and it constantly reorganizes itself to make room for the new things you experience each day.

The first step in memory making is assembling all the different components, says Gina Poe, a neuroscientist who studies memory and sleep at the University of California, Los Angeles. Let's say you're sitting outside under a tree when suddenly a bee stings you. To stash away that not-so-pleasant event, your brain decides that the information about what you were sensing, feeling, thinking, and focusing on before and after the sting is important. It also decides that some of that information is *very* important, like parts of the event that you were paying really close attention to, that were emotional, or that made you feel unsafe. "If something really embarrassing or scary happens, we put a tag on like, 'I would never want this to happen again,'" Gina says.

Next, all that important info from different regions of your mind comes together with help from your hippocampus. (Remember, that's the small, seahorse-shaped part of your brain that helps you learn and navigate.) And during this assembly process, something truly amazing happens: your brain rewires itself, just a little every time.

To stitch together different parts of the experience—like the pain of the sting, where you were, the weather, and lots of other details—into one single memory, your brain creates a tiny network of pulsating neurons that connect those pieces. "That's really what a memory is," Gina says, "the neurons of that network all firing at the same time."

Soon, this new memory moves to your brain's long-term storage facility. The memory gets transferred—usually while you're sleeping—to a brain region called the **CEREBRAL CORTEX**, where it's connected to related memories. That intricate organizational system helps explain why recalling one memory, like the bee sting, often leads to thinking about others, like different experiences you've had near the same tree. It's also one reason why humans are so good

CEREBRAL CORTEX: the large, outermost region of your brain that's crucial for many brain functions, including storing long-term memories

YOUR MEMORY MACHINERY

Memory formation is an all-hands-on-deck situation inside your skull. Memories often involve lots of different kinds of information—facts, sensory data, and emotions among them—so processing and storing all of that requires many areas of your brain to work together as one squishy team. Here are some, but definitely not all, of the many brain parts that help you remember.

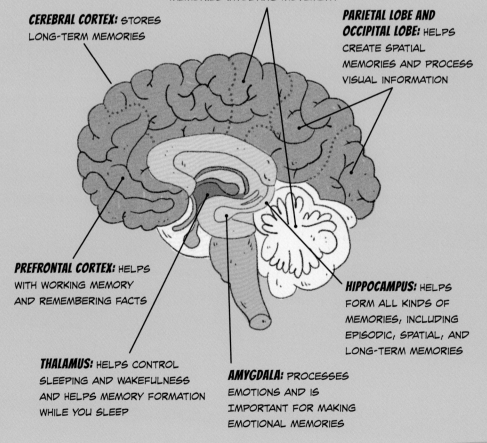

MOTOR CORTEX AND CEREBELLUM: HELPS MAKE MUSCLE MEMORIES AND MEMORIES INVOLVING MOVEMENT

CEREBRAL CORTEX: STORES LONG-TERM MEMORIES

PARIETAL LOBE AND OCCIPITAL LOBE: HELPS CREATE SPATIAL MEMORIES AND PROCESS VISUAL INFORMATION

PREFRONTAL CORTEX: HELPS WITH WORKING MEMORY AND REMEMBERING FACTS

HIPPOCAMPUS: HELPS FORM ALL KINDS OF MEMORIES, INCLUDING EPISODIC, SPATIAL, AND LONG-TERM MEMORIES

THALAMUS: HELPS CONTROL SLEEPING AND WAKEFULNESS AND HELPS MEMORY FORMATION WHILE YOU SLEEP

AMYGDALA: PROCESSES EMOTIONS AND IS IMPORTANT FOR MAKING EMOTIONAL MEMORIES

at building our knowledge by adding new things we've just learned onto stuff we knew before.

But brain rewiring doesn't stop there. Memories can change over time, and their neural networks do, too. When you remember something, the network linking that memory together gets stronger and faster. Neurons get better at sending and receiving signals, and if you recall the memory frequently enough, neurons can grow new bushy dendrites that help zap signals along even faster, making that memory easier and easier to remember in the future.

This process, where your brain's communication networks strengthen the more they're activated, is called **LONG-TERM POTENTIATION**, and it doesn't happen evenly. Which experiences you clearly remember years later depends on what your brain tags as important. If that bee sting brought up big emotions for you, or if you had a severe allergic reaction, those neural pathways would likely get very strong very fast. But if the event wasn't a big deal or if some other much more important thing happened that day—say, an alien landed in your town—you likely wouldn't think about the sting that much. Then, those neural connections would get weaker and weaker, making it harder to recall over time. Decades from now, you'd remember that day as the one with the alien, not the one with the bee sting.

Over time, people forget lots of details about their experiences, and memories can change and get distorted in many different ways. But even though your mind vault isn't perfect, your brain's shape-shifting neural circuitry is one of the fastest and most efficient machines on earth. For squirrels, it also takes lots of networked brainpower and some memory-boosting tricks to find those buried nuts.

LONG-TERM POTENTIATION: the process by which neural connections become stronger the more you use them

MANY FLAVORS OF MEMORY

Just like you have lots of different memories, your brain has many different systems for dealing with the waves and waves of information that are constantly washing over you. Scientists sometimes categorize these systems based on how long we hold on to information—long-term memory, for example, can store info for decades, while short-term memory lets it go in thirty seconds or less. There's also an in-between variety called **WORKING MEMORY**, which kicks in when you repeat new information to remember it. If you've ever used flashcards to learn vocabulary words or said something out loud to keep it fresh, that's your working memory doing its thing. Scientists also categorize memories by type—for instance, if *you* were stashing treats, you would use **EPISODIC MEMORY** to remember the experience of hiding those goodies and **SPATIAL MEMORY** to recall where you hid them and how to get there again.

WORKING MEMORY: the process of retaining information for a short period of time while learning or solving problems

Though researchers still have a lot to learn about how animals' memories work and what information they retain, it's clear that human memory is something that makes us unique. Animals ranging from grizzly bears to frog-eating bats to wasps have short- and long-term memories, but humans have especially powerful working memories that help us add new information to concepts we learned in the past. Some scientists believe that this ability is one reason why humans can do things that require lots of continuous learning—stuff like planning far into the future or speaking complex languages that constantly add new words and meanings—but animals either can't do these things at all or do them in more limited ways.

EPISODIC MEMORY: memory related to experiences you had in the past

SPATIAL MEMORY: memory related to where things, and you, are located

The regions of our brains that are associated with processing memories are uniquely large and well developed, even compared to some creatures with bigger overall brains than ours. But don't let that go to your head. Animals still perform fantastic memory feats—for example, dolphins can recognize dolphins they've met before, even after being separated for more than twenty years. Animals also sometimes beat us in memory challenges: chimpanzees, who also have impressive working memories, have beaten humans at tests that involve predicting a partner's next move and remembering the precise locations of numbers that quickly flash on a screen, though some scientists chalk up the chimps' success to better training, not better brainpower. Head to YouTube to watch a chimp named Ayumu defeat human contenders at this over and over again, helping them remember the feeling of humility one test at a time.

AYUMU'S MOTHER, AI, HELPS RESEARCHERS LIKE TETSURO MATSUZAWA LEARN ABOUT MEMORY IN ANIMALS AND HUMANS.

WELCOME TO SQUIRREL SCHOOL

Like all Squirrel School students, Green is healing and learning at the same time. Green was brought to WildCare's hospital at just four weeks old. She had fallen out of her nest and arrived with a fractured leg. Volunteers splinted her injury and gave her antibiotics and pain medications. Once she was stable, they placed her with a group of other orphaned eastern gray squirrels about the same age. Just like human infants, baby squirrels can't eat solid foods, so every four hours, the WildCare team carefully fed each squirrel formula using a syringe and slowly introduced solid foods, like nuts without shells.

Soon, Green started getting better. A few weeks later, the fracture had healed and her group was old enough to move from an indoor cage to a large

LUCIA AND HER TEAM OBSERVE WILD SQUIRRELS AT THE UNIVERSITY OF CALIFORNIA, BERKELEY.

outdoor enclosure where they could get used to natural sounds and temperatures and learn skills they'd need to survive in the wild, like climbing and cracking acorns on their own.

Here's where Lucia Jacobs comes in. Attached to the squirrels' temporary home is a small tunnel that leads to a second outdoor enclosure Lucia calls an "experimental area." Squirrels can choose to go through the tunnel, and if they do, they'll find a space that looks a lot like the first enclosure, with trees for climbing. This experimental area also has objects to play with, including a wheel squirrels can run on, and it's being watched. Cameras and tracking tags allow researchers to observe these animals and follow their movements without disturbing them.

And soon, Lucia's team will be able to observe even more squirrelly behaviors. She plans to create a section within the experimental area that will have puzzle boxes loaded with food rewards and maybe even fake acorns with devices inside that can measure how squirrels turn and shake nuts they find before burying them.

The goal, she says, is to enable scientists to observe behaviors in ways they can't in a typical indoor lab and to better understand how to help young animals survive in nature. That means studying how squirrels solve problems—like where to bury thousands of nuts and remember where they are later—and what factors influence their decisions. That's why her team is keeping a close eye on Green.

HIDE·AND·SEEK, SQUIRREL STYLE

After moving to her outdoor cage, Green spent two days inching closer and closer to the tunnel, then grabbed a nut with her teeth and cautiously ran through it on day three. Once she was inside the experimental area, she chose where to hide her treasure. Squirrels steal each other's food, so scatter-hoarders

ROBO-RODENTS

Squirrel School is actually part of a much larger squirrel-focused research initiative. Lucia's work centers on behavior, but her team also collaborates with other scientists at different universities who are studying squirrel **BIOMECHANICS**—specifically how these creatures fling themselves through the air like tiny acrobats, make lightning-fast choices about places they can safely land, and how they learn these skills.

The secrets of squirrel movement aren't just interesting to animal scientists. The US Army is funding part of this research in hopes that what scientists learn about squirrel agility can be used to build more nimble robots.

"In robotics, we're extremely jealous of animals," says Dan Koditschek, an engineer at the University of Pennsylvania who is leading the army's squirrel robotics

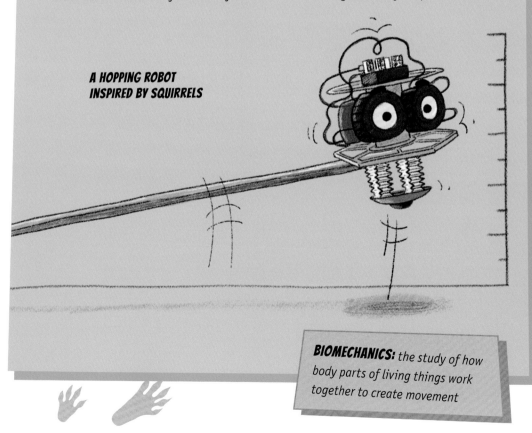

A HOPPING ROBOT INSPIRED BY SQUIRRELS

BIOMECHANICS: the study of how body parts of living things work together to create movement

project. "Our jets can go faster than any animal and our boats can carry much greater loads over the seas than any animal. On any one metric, our technologies are more advanced than animals, but no robot we've ever been able to build can compare even to a cockroach's many different mind and body capabilities."

As of now, robots that deliver aid or help rescue people are slow, clunky, and unable to navigate complicated environments the way rodents do every day. Search-and-rescue robots also can't learn from their mistakes. But, Dan says, squirrels are quick and creative problem-solvers that can easily flit from here to there in a flash. Dan's team is building a mechanical squirrel, one body part at a time. They're building test versions of robotic squirrel paws, legs, and spines, and they plan to keep going. In the future, robots might one day scurry around as quickly and gracefully as the bushy-tailed bio-machines in your own backyard.

like Green need places that are easy for them to remember but hard for others to find.

They have some strategies for doing that. One is by organizing their stashes. Just like you might hide your most precious possession in the very best hiding spot you can think of, squirrels do the same with their food. When squirrels find a nut, they do some tests to figure out how important that food is. Research by Lucia and scientists Mikel Delgado and Stephanie Preston suggests that when a squirrel holds a nut and flicks its head, or when it turns a nut over in its paws or mouth, the squirrel is actually measuring the weight and size of the nut to determine its value.

That value influences where they hide it. Squirrels carefully choose where to store each individual nut and spend more time making sure that really valuable ones are safe. They try to find hiding spots that are safe from potential thieves—these crafty critters sometimes pretend to bury nuts just to throw the competition off—but they also use smells and landmarks to remember where their hiding spots are.

Lucia's lab has shown that squirrels sometimes use a **MNEMONIC DEVICE** called chunking, which involves grouping individual bits of information into categories to make them easier to remember. For squirrels, that means separating nuts by type and burying each variety in its own geographic area—walnuts might get buried in holes near this tree, for instance, while acorns get buried way over there. Humans also use chunking to memorize information: phone numbers separated by dashes,

MNEMONIC DEVICE: *a memory strategy that helps you recall information later*

grocery lists divided by which section of the store the items are in, and library shelves that have one area for mysteries and another for cookbooks are everyday examples.

Mapping and memorizing locations for thousands of nuts is tough, Lucia says, but squirrels are ready: "Their brains literally get bigger when they're making these decisions." Lucia's lab has found that during weeks when a gray squirrel is hiding nuts, its hippocampus actually grows larger, especially in an area called the CA1 subfield, which is important for spatial and episodic memory.

This type of brain growth isn't uncommon in the animal kingdom—many creatures, including you, have brain regions that grow or shrink a little depending on how they're being used. But *when* this growth happens is unusual, she says. For rodents, growth usually happens during breeding times, then their brains shrink some during other times of the year after breeding is over. Squirrels, however, show this growth during weeks when they're storing food, not when they're breeding. That might mean that squirrels direct extra brainpower to find and hide food; then, once they have a firm mental map of their secret snacks, they may not need as many brain resources.

Lucia adds that this research field is full of "mights and maybes." Scientists still have lots of questions about what's happening in the brain when squirrels make food maps, why they abandon or forget about some stashes but not others, and how factors like individual personalities affect decision-making. She hopes that Green and the other furry Squirrel School students can provide new data and ways of thinking about these questions before they're released into the wild to strategically hide acorns in the great big world outside.

ELEPHANTS NEVER FORGET; FISH NEVER REMEMBER. WHAT'S THE TRUTH?

Some animals are famous for their memories, both long and short. Elephants have such strong memories that people often say they never forget, while goldfish are said to retain information for just a few seconds. But is this really true for either animal? Sort of.

Elephants have the largest brains of any land animal on earth—more than three times the weight of ours—and they do have astounding memories, especially when it comes to remembering places, group members, social practices, and family history. Unlike many other animals, elephants can identify and track lots of family members, possibly up to thirty at a time, and can remember spaces and faces they haven't seen for decades.

That long memory is really helpful for survival. For example, during a drought in Tanzania back in the 1990s, researchers noticed that elephant herds that were led by females over age fifty were better at finding food and fresh water than herds led by younger females. Their secret? Older elephants had lived through a similar drought that happened more than thirty years before. Even though they hadn't traveled the drought routes in decades, they remembered where the routes were and passed that information down to young herd members. Elephants do forget things sometimes, but their reputation for having razor-sharp recall mostly rings true.

Goldfish, however, aren't nearly the finned forgetters they're made out to be. Researchers have trained these fish to do lots of tasks, like swimming precise routes, navigating aquatic mazes, and tapping paddles placed in their tanks—all for tasty food rewards, of course. They've found that goldfish retain this training for weeks, months, or potentially even longer after the lessons have stopped.

But perhaps the weirdest testament to the power of these creatures' memories happened at Ben-Gurion University of the Negev in Israel, where scientists built a small robotic car and taught some goldfish how to drive it. The vehicle consisted of a clear tank mounted on a motorized cart, plus a camera, a computer, and tracking equipment to measure the movement of the car and its fish driver. Whenever the fish swam near one of the tank's four walls, the vehicle moved in that direction. After training six fish how to identify a specific target, researchers placed them one by one in the vehicle's tank, put the vehicle inside a white room, and followed along as the gilled motorists drove past obstacles and fake targets to get to the real one (and a snack). In the process, they proved that these fish have longer memories than they get credit for.

CLEAR THE ROAD!
FISH CAR IS COMING
THROUGH.

ACTIVITY
INCEPTION DECEPTION

When you think of storing something, like a winter coat in your closet or a homework assignment on your computer, you probably picture retrieving that thing exactly as it is now sometime in the future. Memories are often described as being "stored" in your mind, but it doesn't happen exactly the same way. Now is your chance to test out how accurate memory really is. This is a two-part activity—you will guide your partner through the first part, and they'll guide you through the second part.

YOU'LL NEED:

- a partner
- some paper and writing utensils

PART 1

1. Tell your partner that you're going to read them a list of words and that they should try to memorize them all.

2. Read the following words out loud: *water, fish, hot, waves, shells, tides, shark, clouds, salty, blue, swimming, seagull, towel, sun, sand*

3. Now give your partner a piece of paper and a pen and ask them to write down all the words they remember as fast as they can.

4. Check their list against the list in step 2. How many words did they remember? Did they write down any words that weren't on the list? Did they forget any words?

All of the words on the list you read aloud are related to beach scenes. The words *beach*, *ocean*, and *sea* weren't actually on the list, but sometimes people "remember" them anyway. Their brains have snuck those words in, even though they weren't part of the memory.

It's actually pretty easy to remember details that didn't happen. When you remember something, your brain reconstructs the memory by activating the neural network connecting individual pieces of it. During that reconstruction process, some details come back stronger than others, and the memory gets a little flexible, allowing you to update it with new information before it gets put back into storage. This flexibility makes it easy for you to string memories together and build your understanding of something over time—just think about a person you've gotten to know better and better over many years. You likely recall early memories of them differently now than you did at the time. During this flexible state, false information can get in there, too, and actually become part of the memory. Now it's your turn to test your memory. Stop reading and pass this book over to your partner.

PART 2

1. Okay, partner. Time for the second part of this activity. Write the following words down on a piece of paper, but don't show anyone else: *house, pencil, apple, shoe, book, flag, rock, train, ocean, hill, music, water, glass, school*

2. Fold your paper so the words are hidden and put it to the side.

3. Tell your partner to listen carefully while you read these words out loud: *pages, letters, school, study, reading, stories, sheets, cover, pen, pencil, magazine, paper, words*

4. When you're done, wait at least five minutes. Feel free to stretch your legs, get a snack, talk about things other than this activity, or do something else entirely.

5. When the wait time is over, give your partner the paper with the list you wrote down in step 1 (the one with *house, pencil, apple,* and *shoe,* among others). Ask them to circle the words that were also in the list you read aloud.

6. Check what they circled. The correct answers are *pencil* and *school,* but people often believe that *book* was also on the read-aloud list.

7. Talk to your partner about the differences between these two exercises. In the first one, the person is asked to remember words they heard read aloud. In the second part, the person is given a list and later asked to circle words they heard. How did each of you do in your exercise? And do you think that the way the exercise was presented and the amount of time you had to wait made a difference in how you performed?

Lots of research shows that how information is presented influences how accurately people remember it. For example, when detectives or police officers question someone who witnesses a crime, how they ask the questions can impact how the witness recalls that event and can contribute to false memories or statements.

BONUS Find a few other people and do both parts of the activity with them. Were memories more accurate in one part of the activity over the other? Do grown-ups perform as well as kids do? You can also create your own false memory challenge. Come up with a theme and write down ten to fifteen words that fit into that theme, but leave a few key ones out. See if your friends remember the words on your list, or if a few new ones sneak into their memories, too.

The second part of this activity is used with the permission of Eric H. Chudler, PhD, Neuroscience for Kids.

CHAPTER 4
HALF-BRAINED BIRDS

STRATEGIC SNOOZING HELPS FEATHERED FRIENDS STAY SAFE.

IN ROCKY, molten fields created by volcanoes, a small brown-and-white bird we'll call Kaia takes flight in the dead of night. Kaia is an ʻakēʻakē (pronounced AH-kay-AH-kay in Hawaiian, or, in English, it's called a band-rumped storm petrel)—a seabird that weighs about as much as a golf ball and nests in high-elevation spots throughout Hawaii.

ʻAkēʻakē are endangered in the United States and only found in Hawaii. More live outside of the US and they're not considered endangered globally, but some conservationists argue that they should be on a worldwide endangered list, too. On the Hawaiian Islands, ʻakēʻakē are fighting for survival, and so are many of the state's other native bird species. Conservationists call Hawaii the extinction capital of the world because the state's rich diversity of plants and animals is much lower today than it used to be. Of the 142 **ENDEMIC** bird species that are native to Hawaii, 95 have died out since humans arrived on the islands, and at least 30 more are endangered.

That's why Bret Nainoa Mossman is looking for birds like Kaia on the state's largest island, which goes by two different names—Hawai'i, spelled similarly to the name of the state, or the Big Island. Bret is a biologist at the Hawai'i Island Natural Area Reserve System who monitors and protects endangered birds. His work involves setting up protective fences and trapping seabird predators, and it requires thinking about how to make people care about these creatures and want to save them. To do that, Bret, who is Native Hawaiian himself, started Birds Hawai'i Past Present—a website (www.birdshawaiipastpresent.com) and social media campaign that posts photos of rare birds, along with information about why they're important to **INDIGENOUS** culture and the challenges the birds face today.

"Birds are a very important foundation of many beliefs and traditions in Native Hawaiian culture," he says. "A lot of the connection that we've had to those birds has been lost. I want to use social media to bring these birds back into our everyday lives."

But finding birds like Kaia isn't easy. 'Akē'akē live in tough-to-reach places, spend much of their time at sea, and, when they're on land, are most active at night. They're even hard to find while they rest. 'Akē'akē sleep in secret spots and may have a neurological trick that helps them avoid unwanted visitors: sleeping with half of their brain alert while the other half rests.

BEASTLY BEDTIMES

People don't function well without enough high-quality sleep—we can be grouchy and moody or have trouble concentrating and remembering things. Our bodies aren't as good at fighting off diseases when we're really tired, and we score much lower on tests. That's a good reason to study ahead of time and get a full night's rest before an exam.

Animals need rest, too, but how much they need, when they sleep, and what happens in their brains during rest varies a lot from species to species. Super sleepers, like koalas, can slumber for twenty hours a day or more, while male fire ants get by on teeny-tiny naps—about 250 every single day, each lasting around one minute. Queen fire ants take fewer, more luxurious six-minute-long snoozes. The perks of being a royal!

Some animals are **DIURNAL**, meaning they sleep at night as we do. Others are **NOCTURNAL** and sleep when it's light out. And a few species don't really fit into either category: for example, the mongoose lemur, a species that lives in the forests of Madagascar and some other nearby islands, is mostly nocturnal during hot, dry months of the year and diurnal during cooler months.

DIURNAL: being active during the day and inactive at night

NOCTURNAL: being active at nighttime and inactive by day

Unlike birds, humans have fairly predictable sleep patterns, and both halves of our brains sleep at the same time. Kids need somewhere between nine to twelve hours of sleep each night to be healthy—exactly how much varies from person to person—while adults need seven to nine hours on average. That's about one-third of your entire life spent in bed! Take your age and divide it by three—that's how many YEARS you've spent asleep.

But don't worry, those hours aren't wasted. While it might feel like your brain is shutting down during sleep, it's actually doing incredibly important jobs, including helping you learn and prepare for the next day. Scientists don't fully understand how exactly your brain does all these tasks—and why people can't sleep half a brain at a time. One way that scientists search for answers is by studying how living things, humans and animals alike, move from light sleep to deep sleep and back again.

ONE-THIRD OF YOUR ENTIRE LIFE IS SPENT ASLEEP.

MEET THE SLIPPERY, SNOT-SHOOTING SEA CREATURE THAT STYMIES SLEEP SCIENTISTS

Scientists usually study sleep in animals and people by measuring brain activity, but that technique doesn't always work for creatures that have very different brains from us. Take the *Cassiopea*, also known as the upside-down jellyfish. This sea dweller hunts by suctioning its bell—the body part that looks like a head—to the seafloor, pointing its tentacles upward and shooting out clouds of toxic, stinging mucus that trap prey. (In fact, this jellyfish can sting you with its snot even if it never touches you.)

Like all jellyfish, *Cassiopea* don't have brains. Instead of having one cranial command center that controls bodily functions and the nervous system (like you have), jellyfish have nerve networks all over their bodies. But even though they don't have brains, at least one study suggests that they still need breaks. At night, they move and respond to movement more slowly, and if they don't get rest, they're less active the next day.

THESE BRAINLESS BLOBS NEED REST JUST LIKE YOU DO.

This study was the first to show that sleep—an activity that we typically think of as requiring a brain—happens in brainless creatures, too, and that even after decades of research on sleep, beings at the bottom of the ocean can still challenge how we think about basic biological processes.

THE NIGHT SHIFT IN YOUR SKULL

Just like there's a rhythm to your days—get up in the morning, eat break-fast, do some activities, then lunch, more activities, dinner, and later bed—there's also a rhythm to your sleep, and it repeats over and over all night long. Tonight, when you snuggle into bed, see if you can feel the transition. As you begin to drift off, your heartbeat and breathing will get slower. Your muscles might twitch a little and it's easy to wake you up. This is the first stage of sleep and it only lasts a few minutes.

Stage two is when the real brain work begins, says neuroscientist Gina Poe. Your body becomes more relaxed, but regions of your brain that are involved in learning and memory get more active. This is the time when some things you've learned during the day get stored in your long-term memory. That means that learning isn't just something that happens when you're awake—getting a good night's rest is a vital part of how much information you remember tomorrow.

Stage two lasts about thirty minutes to an hour, then it's time for deep sleep—stage three—when your brain shifts focus away from keeping you alert and toward getting you ready for the next day. During deep sleep, your brain coordinates cell repair throughout your entire body, and it gets rid of waste chemicals that accumulate in your brain when you're awake. "It's when the heavy-duty cleanup gets done," Gina says, adding that deep sleep usually only happens during the first half of the night.

Finally, it's dream time. Most people spend between ten and thirty minutes in deep sleep, then transition to the last stage, *RAPID EYE MOVEMENT (REM) SLEEP*.

RAPID EYE MOVEMENT (REM) SLEEP: a type of sleep that's characterized by fast, frequent eye movements and increased brain activity

Your brain perks up when it hits the REM stage—in fact, it's almost as active as when you're awake. A lot

WILDEST DREAMS

Have you ever had a dream where you're being chased? Or your teeth are falling out? Maybe you've dreamed that you're flying or falling, or just going about your day doing nothing out of the ordinary. These are some of the most common dreams people have. Many researchers believe that animals dream, too, though it's never been proven.

Mammals, birds, fish, and possibly some reptiles experience REM sleep (or something close to it), and sleeping animals sometimes move as if they're awake—dogs act like they're running during sleep, cuttlefish change color, and octopuses twitch their arms and change the texture of their skin.

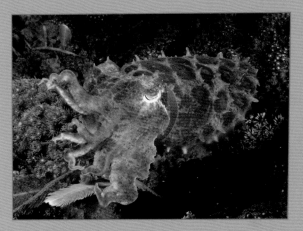

CUTTLEFISH CHANGE COLOR AND TWITCH THEIR ARMS DURING SLEEP.

Some research suggests that animals might dream about the things they experience while they're awake, just like humans do. When rats spent their day running through a maze, their brain activity during REM sleep looked almost identical to when they were doing that action awake. Sleeping zebra finch songbirds have similar brain activity patterns as they do when they're awake and singing.

Scientists are still figuring out what these patterns mean. Maybe they show that the animal is dreaming, or that their brain is storing memories of maze running and singing, or both (or neither). Neuroscientists have a lot of questions about what happens in human brains during sleep, and a lot more questions when it comes to animals.

of dreaming occurs during REM sleep, and it's also a time when your brain processes emotions, stores more memories, and does some neural rewiring. So much important stuff happens while you sleep!

Altogether, one full sleep cycle takes about 105 minutes in the first half of the night and about 90 in the second half. Then your brain goes back to stage two and starts over again. Scientists have researched sleep for a very long time, but there are still lots of questions to untangle: How exactly do different parts of your brain work together to do all of this stuff? Why do humans need to sleep for hours while other animals get by on much less? And why can some creatures, like Kaia, sleep with half their brains, but people can't?

MANY HAWAIIAN NATIVE BIRDS LIKE THIS 'ĀKEPA ARE ENDANGERED.

SLEEP IS (SORT OF) FOR THE BIRDS

In Hawaii, Kaia faces hard challenges. Back before any humans came to the islands, only one land mammal lived there—the Hawaiian hoary bat, which eats insects and isn't a threat to 'akē'akē. Ancient plants and animals evolved without bigger mammal predators around.

The first Polynesian settlers came to the islands sometime between the years 400 and 700, and Hawaii's native birds quickly became a vital part of their religion, culture, and diet. But when European colonizers and traders started arriving in the late 1700s and 1800s, they brought new weapons and diseases Hawaiian people had never encountered before, along with new animals, like ship rats, cats, and mongooses. Native birds suddenly had lots of hungry creatures they hadn't seen before hunting them and their eggs. Without any natural predators of their own, populations of these new animals grew and grew. It wasn't long before bird species, and their ties to indigenous Hawaiian culture, started dying out.

Today, cats, rats, and mongooses are still some of the biggest threats to native Hawaiian birds. 'Akē'akē are small and stealthy, so one of Kaia's best defenses is her ability to hide. One way she stays out of sight is by nesting in spots that are very high up, like steep cliffs and rocky lava fields—places many land-based predators can't reach.

'Akē'akē also evade hungry animals by keeping strange sleep schedules that make it tough for predators—and camera-toting conservationists like

LAVA FIELDS LIKE THIS ONE IN HAWAII VOLCANOES NATIONAL PARK MIGHT NOT LOOK LIKE ANIMAL HABITAT, BUT TO SOME SPECIES OF BIRDS, RODENTS, AND REPTILES, THEY'RE HOME.

Bret—to predict where they're going to be. These birds hunt at sea for weeks at a time, probably dozing right on the water, and when they're on land, "they sleep when they can," Bret says. "They don't have a strong connection to day or night."

Not only is Kaia an unpredictable sleeper; compared to you, she likely wakes up much easier if danger comes lurking, says Niels Rattenborg, a scientist who studies snoozing birds at the Max Planck Institute for Biological Intelligence in Germany. Bird sleep episodes usually last anywhere from a few seconds to around one minute, though this varies by species. It's also likely, though not proven, that Kaia has periods of *UNIHEMISPHERIC SLOW-WAVE SLEEP*, when one of her brain hemispheres sleeps while the other stays alert.

Scientists don't know exactly how many bird species can do this half-brained sleep technique, Niels says. They do know that half-brained sleep allows birds to do some amazing things that humans can't. One is keeping watch. Niels's research shows that when ducks sleep in groups, the ducks on the outer edge do more unihemispheric sleeping than those in the middle. While sleeping, they also keep the eye facing outside the group open, which could mean that these birds use unihemispheric sleep to literally keep an eye out for predators.

This sleep style also helps some birds travel, too. Niels has studied this in great frigatebirds—a species that flies nonstop for days, possibly even months, without landing. Niels's team equipped fourteen of these jet-set birds with devices that recorded brain activity and flight data, then sent them flying across the Pacific Ocean. His team found that the birds took hundreds of naps, each roughly twelve seconds long, while soaring through the sky. Instead of sleeping for eight hours per day like you do, these

UNIHEMISPHERIC SLOW-WAVE SLEEP: a type of sleep where one brain hemisphere rests while the other stays alert

A GREAT FRIGATEBIRD WEARING A FLIGHT RECORDER FOR NIELS'S RESEARCH.

birds slept only about forty minutes total. Though they had periods of sleeping with both brain hemispheres at once—gliding lazily on wind currents—most of the time they used only one, leaving the other alert in case of flight trouble.

Scientists don't know exactly what happens when Kaia sleeps. Based on studies in this area, Niels says that most birds, including 'akē'akē, probably do experience unihemispheric sleep, but more research is needed to verify that. He adds that birds aren't the only unihemispheric sleepers. Certain marine creatures, including species of dolphins, sea lions, and fur seals, also sleep like this, often while swimming. How this process works in animals' brains is "a really big mystery" researchers have yet to unravel, Niels says. "People sometimes write about science as if everything is solved, but really, science is full of questions that are awaiting discoveries."

BIRDS ON THE BRINK

Kaia also has another powerful defense against predators: people like Bret who care about birds. Across Hawaii's Big Island, Bret's team traps native bird

CAN YOU SLEEP WITH HALF A BRAIN?

Humans can't do unihemispheric sleeping, but if you have trouble sleeping in a new place, like at a friend's house or a hotel, it might be because the left side of your brain is actually sleeping a little differently than the right side. Sleeping poorly after arriving in a new place is called the "first-night effect," and scientists have known about it for decades. One small study found that all that tossing and turning might happen because your two brain hemispheres get out of sync: the right side slips into deep sleep while the left side stays in slightly shallower sleep stages.

Researchers are quick to point out that this mental mismatch isn't the same thing that happens in the brains of some birds and other animals. Unlike unihemispheric sleep, the first-night effect usually only lasts for one day, and the differences in activity levels between the two brain hemispheres is much smaller compared to our feathered friends.

But some scientists theorize that our brains slumbering a tad unevenly might suggest that humans are just a little more similar to half-brained sleepers than previously thought. Like birds, ancient humans also needed to watch out for predators, environmental hazards, and lots of other dangers, especially in places they weren't used to yet. Keeping part of the brain a little more alert may have been a protective trait that got passed down from generation to generation.

predators, restores bird-friendly habitats, and monitors bird populations. To learn about how super-secretive 'akē'akē are doing, Bret and his team sometimes become nocturnal themselves: they set up recorders that pick up 'akē'akē sounds throughout the night, then, when they hear something, they head to known burrows and use night-vision equipment to try to spot the birds.

Bret's team can't rescue Hawaii's native birds alone. Saving endangered species requires lots of people, scientists and non-scientists alike, to work together on smart conservation strategies. That means people need to care about the creatures that need saving and to understand why losing native birds means losing a critical piece of Hawaiian history.

To raise awareness about these issues, Bret photographs the native birds he sees and posts them on the Birds Hawai'i Past Present social media channels. He includes their Native Hawaiian names and information about why they're important to the islands' land and Native people. This work, he says, is deeply personal. "In the Hawaiian worldview and in many Indigenous peoples' worldviews, people and nature are one and the same," Bret explains. "Neither can survive without the other. It's like tending to your family."

Kaia is part of that family. Despite the threats that Kaia faces, Bret is hopeful that with time, conservation resources, and attention, 'akē'akē like her can thrive again. Then, he says, he'll also rest easier.

FOR BRET NAINOA MOSSMAN, SAVING SPECIES CAN BE DIRTY WORK.

ACTIVITY
DREAM RECALL CHALLENGE

Scientists have many different theories about why people dream. Some believe that dreaming is part of how long-term memories are formed and stored. Others think that dreaming might be a way for your brain to sort through stress or to simulate and prepare for threatening events. Researchers have many different ideas on *why* we dream, but they agree that dreaming varies a lot from person to person. You might frequently have vivid dreams you can recall in detail the next day, while your next-door neighbor rarely remembers her dreams at all. One person might see color or smell odors in their dreams, while another slips into the same dream every night. How do you dream? This activity is designed to help you notice patterns.

YOU'LL NEED:

- something to write on (this could be some blank paper, an empty notebook, or a document on a computer, smartphone, or tablet)
- a writing utensil
- some patience

PART 1

1. Place your journal and pen right beside your bed.

2. That night, go to sleep just like you normally do. But when you wake up, either in the morning or in the night, immediately write down every single thing you can remember about your dreams. Write it down before you do anything else—people usually forget dreams really quickly after waking up. Think hard about what it looked like in the dream, what you felt, if you had a sense of time, and if you saw any objects or people in your dream that you know in your waking life (or that you don't). You might remember lots of vivid details about your senses or emotions while dreaming or you might not remember dreaming at all. Either way, write down what you can.

3. Repeat step 2 every day for one week.

4. At the end of one week, read through your dream journal and look for patterns. Did certain places, feelings, or colors appear repeatedly in your dreams? Did you do or see things that could never happen in real life? Or were your dreams pretty realistic?

5. On a fresh page, write down any patterns or odd things you notice in your dreams.

Now, let's see if you can influence your dreams. Think about what you do just before falling asleep. Do you read before bed? Or count sheep before you snooze? Maybe you don't really have a relaxing nighttime ritual. In this part of the activity, you're going to change something about what you do before falling asleep and see if that impacts what happens after.

PART 2

6. Pick one simple way you can change what you do before falling asleep, then repeat step 2 every day for one more week with that change in place. You might want to try listening to a particular song or watching a specific video before bed. What happens if you eat a certain food before bed or if you concentrate on your favorite person, color, or piece of clothing while falling asleep?

7. At the end of the week, look at your notes again. How do your dreams this week compare to your dreams the first week? Did you notice changes in what you dreamed about or what kinds of details you were able to remember? Did your dreams look and feel similar week to week, or were there differences in how you felt or experienced the dream? Did you have any control over what happened in your dreams?

**BONUS**

Try changing different pieces of your bedtime routine (just one at a time) or do this activity with a partner and compare notes on any details or patterns you're comfortable sharing.

CHAPTER 5
TIMELESS TORTOISES

SAINT HELENA ISLAND is one of the most remote places in the world. Sitting about 1,200 miles off of the southwestern coast of Africa, this tiny dot of land isn't very well known today, but back before airplanes were invented, it was a different story.

For centuries, Saint Helena was a vital rest stop for ships traveling between Europe and Asia. Diplomats passing through would bring gifts for the island's governor, and exotic animals, especially ones that were easy to keep alive for months at sea, were prized presents. That's likely how Jonathan came to the island. Jonathan is a Seychelles giant tortoise who first set foot on Saint Helena in the 1880s, when he was believed to be about fifty years old. But, unlike the governor he was given to, and the one who came after, and many more after that, this tortoise is still alive.

Jonathan is now the oldest land animal on earth, as far as we know. Clocking in at more than 190, give or take a few years, he was alive before

THIS PHOTO WAS TAKEN IN THE LATE 1800S AFTER JONATHAN (THE TORTOISE ON THE LEFT) ARRIVED ON THE ISLAND.

the internet, television, or gas-powered cars were invented, and he's still in pretty good shape, says Joe Hollins, Jonathan's veterinarian. That's because while Jonathan has a lot in common with people—like his love for neck rubs and human company—"he doesn't really age in the way that we do," Joe says.

Scientists are studying why some species maintain healthy bodies and brains for hundreds of years while others survive for only a few days, but they agree that one key to Jonathan's long life could be hidden in his biological blueprint.

THE SECRET LIVES OF SUPER-AGERS

The definition of "long life" varies a lot across the animal kingdom. For example, mosquitoes hatch and mature into adults in about nine days, and usually die a week or two later. Imagine going from being a newborn all the way to being elderly in just a couple of weeks. For others, aging moves a lot slower: scientists estimate some sea sponges can live 2,300 years, maybe more.

Even animals that look similar can have very different life spans. Many shark species, including great hammerheads, zebra sharks, and grey reef sharks, tend to live up to thirty years, but by that age, Greenland sharks are just getting started. These sharks can survive for an amazing 250 years, and they might even make it all the way to their four hundredth birthday. In fact, scientists don't really know how old Greenland sharks can get—these animals live much longer than the people who study them.

For us humans, living for just one century is incredible. People across the world live about 74 years on average, but a very small number reach age 115 or more. What's their secret? And why don't people live as long as Greenland sharks?

Scientists ask these questions, too. Many different things influence how long a person or animal lives and how healthy they stay throughout their life: diet, exercise, rest, social connections, safety, stress, habitat,

GREENLAND SHARKS LIKE THIS ONE ARE SOME OF THE OLDEST ANIMALS ON EARTH.

and how well they resist and fight off diseases all factor in. The choices we make and the environments we live in greatly affect our life spans, but another piece of the puzzle lies inside our cells, says Steve Austad, a biologist at the University of Alabama, Birmingham, who studies how animals and people age.

Your cells contain a very long, very tiny set of instructions for how to make you. You've probably heard of this microscopic manual before—it's called DNA, which is short for *DEOXYRIBONUCLEIC ACID*. (What a mouthful! It's pronounced dee-OKS-see-rye-bo-noo-KLAY-ik ASS-id.)

DNA molecules are shaped like long ladders that have been twisted around and around, and pieces of them, called *GENES*, carry instructions for

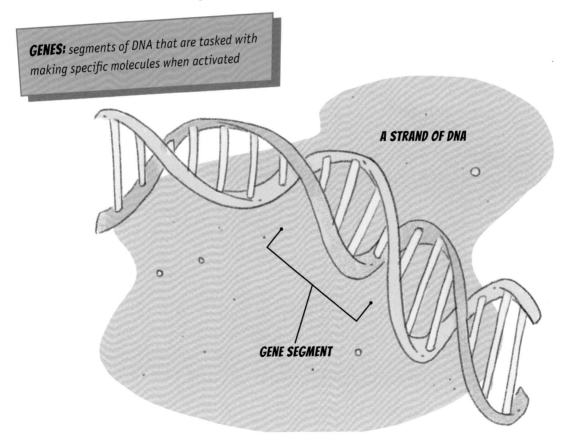

A STRAND OF DNA

GENE SEGMENT

Your body has a lot of DNA squeezed into a very tiny space. If you extracted all the DNA from just one of your cells, uncoiled it, and laid it end to end, it would be about as tall as a large refrigerator. Stretch out all of the DNA in your entire body and you'd have a strand that's billions of miles long—more than enough to stretch from the sun all the way to Pluto and back.

making molecules that your body uses to build and run everything from your tissues, muscles, and blood vessels to your hair, bones, teeth, and organs.

Some genes, and combinations of genes, are responsible for making physical features you can see, like your skin tone and the shape of your hands; others are responsible for your internal systems, including your brain and the many, many processes it operates. Genes work together, almost like a complicated microscopic symphony. They turn on to produce materials only when your body needs them—scientists call this **GENE EXPRESSION**, and your phenomenal brain has more active, expressing genes than any other part of your body.

Genes make species unique. They determine whether an organism will become a person, a flower, or a woolly mammoth, and they determine many differences between individuals in the same species, like which people have naturally curly hair, who's born with brown eyes, and even whether you like certain foods. For example, one tiny tweak to your genes and the taste of an herb called cilantro could go from herby to soapy. Gross!

Genes carry blueprints for building all sorts of extraordinary biological defenses

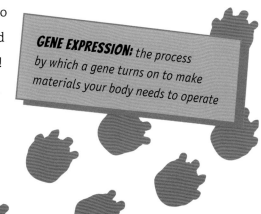

GENE EXPRESSION: the process by which a gene turns on to make materials your body needs to operate

that help long-lived species survive for years and years, explains Steve. Some species can repair their own cells in ways that other animals can't. Others can resist cancers or conditions that reduce brain function, change the way that their bodies use energy, or even alter their own DNA.

Steve is on a quest to learn how creatures pull off these impressive life-extending feats. He studies many different species but especially focuses on two extremely old ones—the ocean quahog clam, which can survive more than five hundred years, and a small, tube-like water creature called a hydra that grows a brand-new body about every three weeks and shows "absolutely no signs of aging," Steve says. According to one study, hydras living in controlled, predator-free environments might be able to live 1,400 years or more. "It's a very unusual case," Steve adds.

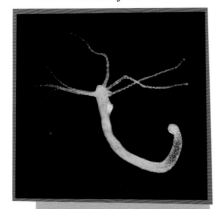

DAMAGED PART? NO PROBLEM. THIS HYDRA REGENERATES BODY PARTS WHEN IT GETS HURT.

Jonathan the tortoise is also unusual. Some scientists believe that DNA from him and other long-lived species can help uncover why some people and animals live an unusually long time.

BODIES IN FLUX

Jonathan wasn't always an aging icon. When Joe Hollins first arrived on Saint Helena back in 2009, he wasn't sure if Jonathan would survive for the next few years. No veterinarians were living on the island at that time, and the four tortoises that resided at the governor's estate didn't have easy access to fresh water or good medical care.

IMMORTALITY UNDER THE SEA

Can you imagine being able to live your life all over again, starting as a baby? One jellyfish can. *Turritopsis dohrnii*—nicknamed the "immortal jellyfish"—is a species that's smaller than a pencil eraser and lives in shallow warm waters throughout the world. When it gets hurt or enters a harsh environment, *T. dohrnii* absorbs its tentacles back into its body. Then it does the same thing that brand-new jellyfish larvae do—it sinks to the seafloor (or nearest hard surface), attaches itself there, and sprouts a stalk called a polyp, which can clone itself again and again. This polyp colony grows bigger and bigger, then eventually blooms, releasing new jellyfish that are identical to the one that was hurt.

    T. dohrnii can perform this death-defying feat over and over again. Although they're still vulnerable to predators, diseases, and environmental hazards, some researchers call them biologically immortal because it's not clear how long they could live under perfect conditions. It's also unclear exactly why these jellyfish can revert back to their youth while other species can't. While scientists are aware of some things that make *T. dohrnii* DNA different from that of other species—like extra copies of genes that deal with maintaining and protecting DNA—answers, for now, are as slippery as the jellyfish themselves.

THESE TEENY-TINY JELLYFISH MIGHT HOLD THE SECRET TO IMMORTALITY.

Jonathan was skinny. His beak should have been dense and tough, but instead, it was soft, making it difficult for him to eat grass. He was blind, had trouble finding food, and would try to eat anything nearby. After seeing Jonathan eat mouthfuls of dirt, "I thought he was pretty much on his last leg," Joe says. "Basically, he was starving to death."

Joe leaped into action. He rearranged the tortoises' habitat so they could access fresh water more easily, and he put them on a new diet that included grasses the tortoises had already been eating along with a weekly treat of fresh vegetables and a little fruit—cucumbers and cabbage are Jonathan's favorites. Slowly, Jonathan got better. He gained weight, became more active, and his beak regrew, letting him graze throughout the day.

BATH TIME! JOE CLEANS OFF JONATHAN'S SHELL.

And he's thrived ever since. Jonathan shows signs of aging—aside from his loss of sight, he also can't smell very well and moves even more slowly than he once did—but otherwise, he's still pretty healthy, even though he's nearly two hundred years old.

Jonathan's environment is one major reason why he's survived so long, Joe says—the governors' tortoises have always been protected from predators and since 2009 have received top-notch nutrition and care. Another major reason is his genes. But before diving into how Jonathan's genes slow down aging, let's talk about what aging is and how it affects people.

You're aging this very second. Humans spend the first few decades of life growing up: that means getting taller and developing more strength, bone mass, muscles, hair, immunity, thinking abilities, and so on. Most people reach full maturity around age twenty-five to thirty. Then, as they enter their forties, fifties, and sixties, muscles and bones shrink, hair turns gray, wrinkles appear, vision and hearing might get duller, and people become more vulnerable to infections, among lots of other changes.

Our brains also transform over time. When you were very young, your brain was a network-building machine that could form thousands and thousands of new neural connections every single second. By age six, your brain was almost the same volume as an adult's—about 90 percent of the way there—and it's still growing today. But when people enter their thirties and forties, their brains start to shrink, just a little at a time and in some places more than others.

Shrinking often happens in two brain regions that are crucial for memory: the hippocampus, which helps memories form, and the cerebral

OUR BRAINS TRANSFORM OVER TIME.

cortex, which stores long-term memories. Researchers believe that this shrink-age is likely one reason why older people often have more trouble remembering new information and doing tasks that involve certain types of memories. For example, elderly people sometimes have slower working memory or difficulty recalling details of things they experienced long ago, but they usually don't have any trouble remembering skills they've done so frequently that they're almost automatic—activities like tying a shoe or playing a musical instrument.

These brain and body transformations happen because our DNA and cells accumulate damage and, over many years, don't function as well as they used to. In the brain, for example, the magnificent network of electric neural communication often gets weaker in old age—some neurons die off or retract some of their bushy, branch-like dendrites, which breaks connections with neurons. Other nerve cells send and receive signals less efficiently over the decades. Cells throughout the body might lose their ability to resist infections or empty out waste products.

Aging also has its benefits—studies show that older people are generally happier and less stressed than younger folks and that they often perform just as well in jobs that require lots of complex thinking.

There are many things that kids and adults can do to stay healthy through-out their lives—eating healthy, wearing sunscreen, exercising, and avoiding cigarettes are just a few—but our genes also play a role in how we age, and we don't have nearly as much control over them.

BLUEPRINTS FOR SURVIVAL

Your genes come from your biological parents. Your cells each contain roughly twenty thousand pairs of genes—half of each pair comes from one parent, half from the other—and they're a major reason why biologically connected families often share similar physical traits, like skin tone or dimples, and why some health conditions might "run in the family."

Genes are also a key reason why some people live longer, Steve Austad says. Some gene combinations are better than others at suppressing tumors, fighting infections, or keeping organs and tissues healthy, but figuring out exactly what those combinations are or how they extend a person's life span is tough. Only some of the traits our genes carry actually show up in our bodies, and it's often impossible to predict if a person will inherit a specific gene from one parent or how that gene will function when paired with a match from the other parent.

Plus, genes aren't the only things that influence aging, Steve adds. Compare individuals in the same species (say, one human to another human or a fly to another fly), and typically only about one-quarter of the difference in life span can be chalked up to differences in genes.

"Most people think that you can't live a long time unless you have long-lived parents," he says. "Having long-lived parents is certainly very helpful, but it's only 25 percent of all of the variation in human longevity."

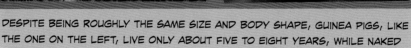
DESPITE BEING ROUGHLY THE SAME SIZE AND BODY SHAPE, GUINEA PIGS, LIKE THE ONE ON THE LEFT, LIVE ONLY ABOUT FIVE TO EIGHT YEARS, WHILE NAKED MOLE RATS (RIGHT) CAN LIVE THIRTY YEARS OR MORE.

AGING BY THE NUMBERS

The average human lives to about 74 years. Here's how the typical human stacks up to average life spans in the wild.

LADYBUG:
2–3 years

PORCUPINE:
5–7 years

EMPEROR PENGUIN:
15–20 years

BOTTLENOSE DOLPHIN:
45–50 years

MONORHAPHIS CHUNI
SEA SPONGE: unknown,
possibly up to 11,000 years

CLOWN FISH: 8 years

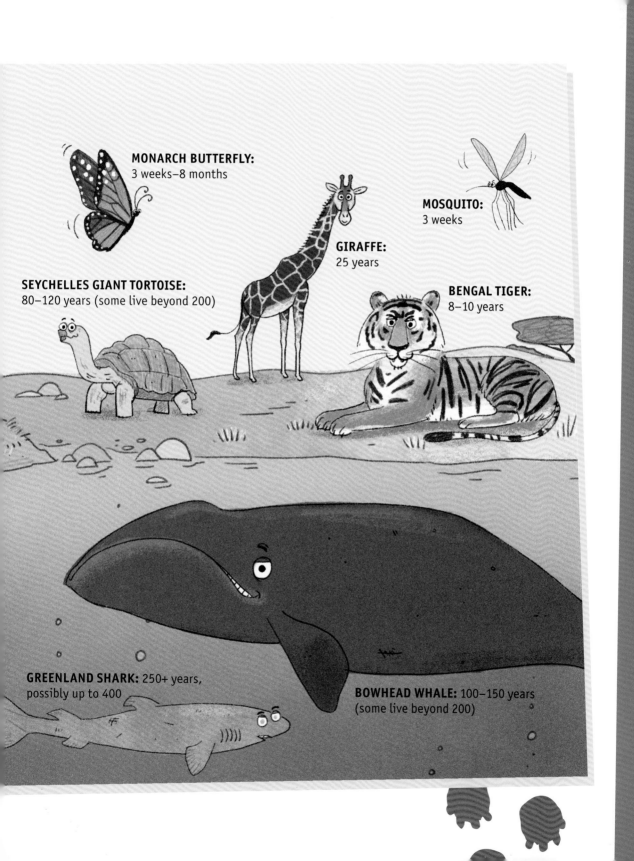

MONARCH BUTTERFLY:
3 weeks–8 months

MOSQUITO:
3 weeks

GIRAFFE:
25 years

SEYCHELLES GIANT TORTOISE:
80–120 years (some live beyond 200)

BENGAL TIGER:
8–10 years

GREENLAND SHARK: 250+ years,
possibly up to 400

BOWHEAD WHALE: 100–150 years
(some live beyond 200)

Other factors, like lifestyle and environment, make up the rest. But compare two different species, like a human and a Seychelles giant tortoise, and genetic differences account for "probably about 99 percent" of why one species lives so much longer, he says.

So what makes Jonathan's genes so special? Scientists are looking for a definitive answer, but here's what they do know: Jonathan doesn't look a lot like you (unless, of course, you also have scaly, greenish skin and a tough shell), but his genes aren't really that different from yours.

Giant tortoises have about 90 percent of the same genes that you do, but in different numbers. Compared to humans, giant tortoises have more copies of certain genes that protect and heal. That includes extra copies of genes that repair cells after they get damaged and of genes that prevent tumors from forming, which helps explain why tortoises get cancer far less frequently than people do. Jonathan also has more copies of genes that strengthen his immune system. For instance, most mammals have only one copy of a gene called PRF1, which is important for making cells that fight viruses and infections. Giant tortoises, however, have twelve copies of this gene.

Studies on other kinds of animals might also reveal possible reasons why Jonathan's brain ages differently from ours. Some research on geckos suggests that reptiles might lose brain neurons at a slower rate than people do, though more studies are needed to prove that conclusively. Other research on our closest animal relatives shows that not all brains shrink with age: in one study that used brain-imaging tools to compare humans and chimpanzees, apes young and old had roughly the same brain volume, but young people had brains that were significantly bigger—in some regions, as much as 25 percent bigger—than older people's.

Steve believes that Jonathan's slow pace might also have something to do with his longevity. Giant tortoises move slowly and age slowly, and, thanks to their genes, their bodies burn energy much more slowly than ours do. For instance, your heart beats somewhere between sixty and one hundred times per minute, but Jonathan's beats only about six times per minute, which requires a lot less energy. Steve says that animals that burn energy slowly, like giant tortoises and Greenland sharks, often live longer on average than similar species that move and burn energy faster. But there are also lots of exceptions: sloths move and burn energy more slowly than almost anything on earth, but wild ones only survive about twenty years.

While scientists like Steve search for answers that could one day extend human life, Jonathan is plodding toward his next birthday. If he makes it, he'll break the Guinness World Record (again) for the oldest turtle or tortoise that's ever lived. Joe will be ready to celebrate with yummy treats. Then it's back to doing what Jonathan does best: taking life one slow, steady day at a time.

FOR JONATHAN, SLOW AND STEADY WINS.

HISTORY HUNTER

While other scientists use genetic analysis to understand how people might age more slowly in the future, Gretchen Johnson uses it to uncover the past. Gretchen is a geneticist who studies ancient DNA—genetic material from people who lived thousands, or even millions, of years ago—and a few years back, she stumbled onto a treasure trove of it on Saint Helena.

At the time, the Saint Helena government was building the island's first airport in an area called Rupert's Valley. But when construction workers started digging into the soil, they found something mysterious: two human skeletons. A team of archaeologists came to the island to figure out how many more graves were beneath the land set aside for the airport, and the more they investigated, the more they found. For ten

GRETCHEN JOHNSON UNCOVERS LOST HISTORIES USING ANCIENT DNA.

weeks, scientists unearthed skeleton after skeleton—325 in total, with thousands more believed to be buried throughout the surrounding valley. Who were these people, and why were they buried without any grave markers?

Rupert's Valley is next to Rupert's Bay, a coastal spot that played an important role in Saint Helena's history. The island was declared a British territory in the 1600s and for centuries served as a rest stop for trade ships that were traveling from Africa to Europe and North or South America. Many ships were transporting enslaved people under horrifying, inhumane conditions. When England outlawed slave trading in the 1800s and ended slavery in Saint Helena and other British-run colonies, the British Navy soon began seizing ships that wouldn't comply. But they didn't have an ethical plan for what to do with the captured, now free, people on board, many of whom were children. They brought some of them to Saint Helena.

Between 1840 and the late 1860s, tens of thousands of newly freed people were brought to a British navy site set up on Rupert's Bay. Many died during the trip or soon after arriving and were buried in the valley nearby, with no information on who they were, where they came from, or what they experienced in life. Among those who survived, more than eighteen thousand left Saint Helena and landed in places across the world, including the Caribbean, South Africa, and the southern United States—and not much is known about what happened to them either.

GRETCHEN AT THE GOVERNOR'S ESTATE ON SAINT HELENA

More than 170 years later, Gretchen is working to uncover their lost histories. In 2018, she flew to Saint Helena to collect DNA from the skeletons archaeologists discovered in Rupert's Valley, which are being kept above ground until a burial site is created. Ancient DNA is tough to get—tissues, organs, and muscles all break down pretty fast—so Gretchen relied on the petrous bone, which sits deep inside your ear and protects the fragile organs that help you hear and stay balanced. Because it's one of the toughest, densest bones in your entire body, it decays slowly, preserving the cells inside for a long time, sometimes millions of years.

GRETCHEN IN THE LAB ON SAINT HELENA

Gretchen took cells from the skeletons' petrous bones, and she's using the DNA inside to learn about the people they once were. By comparing her samples to DNA from other places throughout the world, Gretchen can trace where each person lived before coming to Saint Helena, and she can gather clues about the details of their lives, like what foods they ate and what diseases they encountered. Together, Gretchen's data tell a story about how thousands of people came to one of the world's most remote islands and what happened to them before and after they got there.

"It's like this missing part of world history. More than twenty-six thousand people arrived on the island and no one had any idea they were there," she says. "It's very cool to try to piece together the story."

Gretchen adds that this story continues through the living descendants of those who passed through Saint Helena. Shining light on this forgotten piece of history

could help people today learn more about the story of their own family and about relatives from long ago that they never knew they had. Gretchen sometimes wonders if that might include her. Gretchen's family is from Jamaica, a Caribbean country formerly ruled by Great Britain where thousands of freed people landed after leaving Saint Helena.

"When I was first researching this, diving deeply, I said, 'Oh, my goodness, this is so interesting. What if this is one of my long-lost ancestors?'" she says. "There's so much to learn."

A MEMORIAL TO THE FREED PEOPLE WHO ARE BURIED IN RUPERT'S VALLEY

ACTIVITY
DNA DETECTIVES

Each of your cells contains two copies of each of your genes, but some living things have more copies. Strawberry cells, for example, contain eight copies of their genome. That means that there's a whole lot of DNA crammed into each cell. In this activity, you'll get to see some of that DNA for yourself.

YOU'LL NEED:

- 1 resealable plastic bag
- 2 medium or large strawberries with any green leaves removed (you can use fresh or frozen ones, but thaw any frozen ones before starting the activity)
- 1 teaspoon of liquid dish detergent
- ½ teaspoon of salt
- ¼ cup of water
- 2 clear cups
- 1 coffee filter
- 1 spoon
- Some cold rubbing alcohol. Make sure you have at least ¼ cup—take a peek at your bottle and use your best guess. No need to measure the rubbing alcohol out ahead of time. To get the alcohol cold, put the bottle in your freezer an hour or two before you start the experiment.

1. Put the strawberries into the plastic bag, seal it, and gently smash it in your hands until the strawberries are completely crushed. This starts to break open the cells and release the DNA.

2. In one plastic cup, add the dish detergent, salt, and water, and mix together with the spoon.

3. Open the bag and add 2 teaspoons of this mixture in. Push as much air out of the bag as you can and reseal it.

4. Gently crush the bag in your hands for another minute. The detergent in this mixture will continue to break the strawberry cells open, releasing the DNA, while the salt separates the DNA from proteins in the cell. Make sure that the contents of the bag are mixed thoroughly, but try to avoid making a lot of soapy bubbles if you can. (A few are fine.)

5. Unfold the coffee filter and place it inside the unused plastic cup. You're going to pour the mixture in for the next step, so make sure that the filter is open and that the cup can catch any liquid that's poured into the filter.

6. Now open the bag and pour the mixture into the filter. The filter should catch the solid particles and allow the liquids to seep through into the cup. Wait a few minutes for it to seep, then twist the top of the filter to form a little pouch and squeeze it to release even more liquid into the cup.

7. Look at how much liquid you have. Carefully angle the cup a little and slowly pour an equal amount of cold rubbing alcohol down the inside of the cup (you probably won't need much). Don't mix or stir it.

8. Set the cup completely upright and watch. In a few seconds, you should see some cloudy, white stuff form on top. That small glob of gooey stuff is DNA—the alcohol makes it clump together and separate from the strawberry mixture. You can even try to pull it out with the end of your spoon or with a toothpick.

Did anything surprise you about the DNA? Were you surprised by how it looked? Or by its texture? Or by how much of it came out of two strawberries? You might have been surprised that strawberry DNA is milky white and not red like many strawberries themselves.

BONUS Try this experiment using different kinds of fruit—bananas and kiwi work particularly well. Just remember to remove the skin so the fruit is soft and squishable.

This activity was adapted with permission from the National Human Genome Research Institute. © 2022. All rights reserved.

CHAPTER 6
CHATTY CETACEANS

OFF THE COAST of a tiny island in the Caribbean, a whale named Pinchy makes a special clicking noise to call her family. Pinchy is enormous—female sperm whales like her weigh about as much as seventeen cars stacked on top of each other, and males weigh twice that. Her clicks can be equally impressive. Sperm whales have incredible vocal control and can produce soft clicks or, occasionally, clicks powerful enough to accidentally burst your eardrum if you happen to be close by.

Many marine animals use vocal clicks to locate objects or other creatures. Scientists call this **ECHOLOCATION**, and Pinchy does it, too, to hunt and map her surroundings. But unlike dolphins and some other whale species, sperm whales also make a different type of click, called a **CODA**, that they use to communicate and socialize with each other.

ECHOLOCATION: the process of emitting sound waves and using echoes reflected back to determine the locations of things

CODA: special clicks whales produce that are used for communication, rather than for echolocation

What Pinchy doesn't know, as she sends out her codas, is that she's being tracked and recorded—and that somewhere miles away, scientists will use those sounds to try to figure out how to speak whale.

DID YOU KNOW?

Whales have the largest brains in the animal kingdom. Weighing roughly the same as a large watermelon, a sperm whale's brain is about six times larger than yours. Size isn't everything—even with tinier brains, humans can still do lots of tough tasks that whales can't. But some research suggests that animals with big brains, compared to the size of their bodies, are more likely to have ways of communicating and socializing that are similar to how humans do those things. That could help explain why whale vocalizations are so complex.

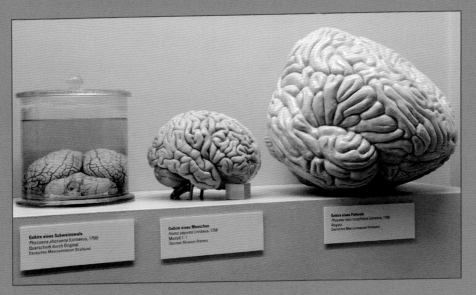

FROM LEFT TO RIGHT, A PORPOISE BRAIN AND MODELS OF A HUMAN BRAIN AND A SPERM WHALE BRAIN

COMMUNICATIVE CREATURES

If you've ever wondered why your cat meows loudly or why birds tweet the way they do, you're not alone. Humans have spent centuries trying to decode what animals around us are saying when they bark, grunt, cluck, croak, or coo. Sounds that humans or animals make with their voices to communicate are called **VOCALIZATIONS**, and they're not the only way creatures get their messages across. Just like us, animals communicate in many different ways—gestures, body language, and facial expressions are just a few—but they also have methods that humans don't typically use, like sending messages with smelly chemicals. Animals might use vocalizations to let others know that food or predators are nearby or to announce, *Hey! This area is mine.*

Scientists debate whether these sounds count as language, but many think that they don't. Vocal languages humans use are made up of individual sounds that can be changed and combined, following grammar rules, to convey information. People often communicate the same types of messages animals do—for example, you'd probably warn someone if you thought they were in danger. But humans also talk about all sorts of things we aren't experiencing at the moment, like past events, future ones, fictional ideas, and even big philosophical questions. We also create and learn new words over time.

Animal vocalizations are more limited. As far as scientists know, animals can't combine individual sounds to create an infinite number of messages in the same way that we can, and their calls typically only relay simple information about things happening right in front of them. But there's also research that challenges those rules. For example, some studies indicate that certain species of songbirds have their own bird grammar. Other experiments show that mother orangutans will wait

VOCALIZATION: communication sounds that humans or animals make using their respiratory systems

SAY WHAT?

Vocalizations are one way to get messages across, but animals also have lots of other strategies. Here are some of the wilder ways that animals send messages:

BUBBLE TROUBLE

To stick with their group, herring turn to an unusual communication source. These salt-water fish move together in large schools and might relay messages through farts. There aren't a lot of studies on herring flatulence, but the research that does exist 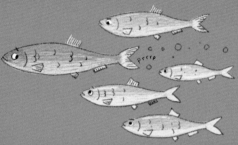 shows that these creatures release air bubbles through their fishy butts when they're scared or when they're moving upward or downward in the water. They also emit different bubble patterns when night falls, leading scientists to think that farting might be one way that these fish stay together when it's harder to see.

GOOD VIBES

Elephants are famous for their blasting trumpeting noises, but they communicate in ways that people can't hear, too. Elephants make rumbling sounds, most of which are outside of the range that human ears can hear. These rumbling sound waves travel  through the air and the ground, creating vibrations that fellow elephants miles away can detect with their sensitive feet. Using sound and vibrations together, the world's largest land animals can chat without nearby humans knowing.

DANCE OR DIE

Many male animals use dances to impress females they'd like to mate with, including peacock spiders. A spider starts his dance by raising his third pair of legs to the sky and fluttering them in the air. Eventually, his abdomen pops up, radiating shades of blue, red, green, and orange as he weaves his way over. There's a lot on the line—if a female peacock spider doesn't like a male's dance, she might eat the performer.

NICE POO MEET YOU

To learn some fast facts about their fellow rhinos, white rhinoceroses head to giant piles of poop. Rhino poop is packed with chemicals that distinguish the age, sex, and health of each animal as well as information about whether they're ready to mate. Many spe-

cies leave similar chemical messages in their poop and pee, but rhinos make pooping a team sport. Groups poop in the same spot and their poos pile up in mounds called middens that can be up to 65 feet (20 meters) across—about the length of a semitruck. These poo piles act a little like rhino social media—in just one spot, these animals can learn about what's going on in their community.

until after a predator is gone, sometimes for up to twenty minutes, before letting out alarm calls to warn their babies—proving that in some circumstances, these great apes can verbally communicate about events in the recent past.

Though researchers debate what findings like these mean, everyone agrees on one thing: no animal on earth uses language like humans do. Scientists believe that the way that our brains grew and changed over millions of years is a major reason why our spoken languages are much more sophisticated and complex compared to animal vocalizations.

Rodrigo Braga, a neuroscientist at Northwestern University in Evanston, Illinois, studies parts of the human brain that are bigger today than they were a few million years ago. He says that both you and your early, early, early ancestors have distinct brain regions that process information from each of your senses. For example, the visual cortex of your brain, which is located near the back of your skull, interprets signals sent from your eyes, allowing you to see. Likewise, the auditory cortex is on each side of your brain and interprets signals you hear. Scientists call these areas **UNIMODAL** because they mostly deal with information from just one sense.

UNIMODAL AREA: an area of the brain that primarily deals with information from one sense

But over the past few million years, human brains have changed, especially in spots that are between unimodal areas. Scientists call these spots **TRANSMODAL** because they don't deal with information from one sense alone. "One thing that makes the human brain unique is that the areas between all of those unimodal regions have expanded so much," Rodrigo says, adding that scientists believe these transmodal areas are important for processing and understanding

TRANSMODAL AREA: an area of the brain that deals with information that isn't tied to a single sense

language. "You can hear language and you can write language. One is visual and one is auditory, but you're still using language. It's beyond any one sense."

Those larger transmodal regions might help explain why human language is so extraordinary, but that isn't definite. Scientists are still learning about language in both animals and people, and some researchers are searching for links between the two.

PINCHY'S PLIGHT

Pinchy began contributing her codas to science in 2005. Back then, a whale researcher named Shane Gero and a team of marine scientists started following sperm whales near the Caribbean island of Dominica in hopes of learning more about how these creatures live, behave, and communicate. Sperm whales live in families that are made up of female whales and their calves; teenage males leave the group and usually don't come back.

SHANE GERO (IN THE BLUE SHIRT) AND HIS TEAM TAGGING WHALES

DIALECT: *a form of a language that is used in a particular part of the country or by a particular group of people*

Codas help these families recognize one another. These sounds change from region to region and sometimes from group to group. Just as people who speak the same language might use different words, accents, or grammar rules depending on what part of the world they're from, whales have local **DIALECTS**, too. For example, sperm whales recorded in areas of the Pacific Ocean near Chile emit codas that sound different from sperm whales recorded off the coast of Japan. Whales living in the same place can also have different dialects, Shane says. Our towns and cities are filled with groups of people who speak the same language in unique ways, and the same is often true in whale communities under the sea.

Like humans, whales aren't born with these dialects—calves learn coda patterns from their family members and use them within their social groups. Sperm whale families often spend time with other whales that have the same coda dialect, sometimes even babysitting each other's calves, and they stay away from individuals with different dialects.

In 2005, Shane and scientists in Dominica had lots of questions about sperm whales, including when and why whales use codas. They started making recordings and called their research initiative the Dominica Sperm Whale Project. Pinchy and the six others in her family were among the first whales recorded. The scientists nicknamed them the Group of Seven.

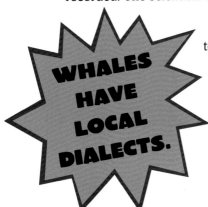

WHALES HAVE LOCAL DIALECTS.

Since then, the Dominica Sperm Whale Project team has spent roughly five thousand hours hanging out with whale families, like Pinchy's, giving scientists around the world a peek into the lives of whales. They know, for example, that Pinchy already had

HOWDY, TOP O' THE MORNING, OR G'DAY, MATE?

Whales aren't the only animals with dialects. Some bird species like the hermit thrush sing differently depending on whether they're in the eastern or western parts of North America. Fruit bats, wolves, and other mammals, like the rock hyrax, which looks a bit like a gopher or prairie dog, also have different calls from region to region. It's likely that many more species have dialects, too, but scientists just haven't studied them yet. That could change in the future, though. Dialects can give researchers valuable information they can use to study how certain species evolved and split into different populations, and to improve conservation plans for threatened or endangered animals.

a young calf, named Scar, and that she gave birth to another, named Tweak, in 2008. They know that Pinchy's group hangs out with a neighboring family that scientists call The Utensils—they named individual whales in that group Knife, Fork, Can Opener, and Hope—and that a new calf was spotted with both groups in 2021. It's not clear if Pinchy or a different whale is the parent. Scientists also know that sperm whale numbers are dropping in the Caribbean, Pinchy's family included. Today, only three members of the original Group of

SCIENTISTS CAN ALSO IDENTIFY WHALES BY THEIR TAILS' UNIQUE SHAPES AND NOTCHES. THESE TAILS ALL BELONG TO WHALES INVOLVED IN THE DOMINICA SPERM WHALE PROJECT.

Seven remain. The rest have either left the group or died.

In 2017, a marine scientist named David Gruber partnered with two computer scientists—Shafi Goldwasser and Michael Bronstein—and came up with an idea for a new way to use the whale recordings. What if they fed the recordings and data about the whales into a software program that's designed to find sound patterns? Could a computer quickly identify individual whales? And, if so, could it uncover insights about whale communication that humans haven't yet discovered?

They partnered with Shane's Dominica team and called their new research program Project CETI, which stands for the **CETACEAN** Translation Initiative. They weren't sure if their approach would work. Other researchers had tried this kind of thing before, using vocalizations from whales and other species, but none had been truly successful. One reason is that learning a language is really tough, for people and computers.

CETACEAN: *a classification of mostly large marine mammals that includes whales, dolphins, and porpoises*

THAT'S WHALE FOR *HELLO*

Scientists have many different ideas about how humans learn languages, but one way is by attaching a new word to an object or concept and repeating that association over and over again. For example, if you say "spoon" while

TO GATHER LOTS AND LOTS OF DATA, SCIENTISTS ATTACH SENSORS THAT TRACK AND RECORD WHALES AS THEY MOVE THROUGH THE OCEAN.

showing a spoon to someone who doesn't speak your language, with enough repetitions that person will know what that word means.

Some computers learn in similar ways, says Jacob Andreas, a Project CETI scientist who's helping to create computer programs that could help decode what whales are saying. Computer systems that do jobs that typically require human intelligence and problem-solving are called **ARTIFICIAL INTELLIGENCE**, or AI for short. Many AI systems use data and instructions from humans to make decisions that are in line with a specific set of goals. You probably encounter AI every single day. For instance, whenever you watch a video online, then see recommendations for similar content, that's AI using the video you picked to make choices about what else you might enjoy.

AI appears in all kinds of places—everywhere from video games to medical diagnoses to military weapons—and language translation is no exception. Teaching an AI system how to

ARTIFICIAL INTELLIGENCE (AI): computer systems that can do things that are commonly associated with human intelligence

translate usually requires inputting lots of samples of one language along with known translations that the system can learn from, Jacob says. But that's not possible with animal vocalizations: "We don't have correspondences between words in English and words in whale-ese."

Instead, Jacob's team is training AI systems to do two major tasks. The first is separating recordings of codas, which whales often emit in social situations, from echolocation clicks, which are used for hunting and navigation. The second is a task made possible fairly recently by the Dominica Sperm Whale Project.

Scientists have long had vocalization recordings, but they usually don't have information on what was happening when the animal made that sound.

SHANE'S TEAM HAS IDENTIFIED MORE THAN 20 DIFFERENT WHALE FAMILIES, LIKE THIS ONE, THAT VISIT THE WATERS NEAR DOMINICA.

Thanks to the project's detailed data collection, Jacob's team can pair coda recordings with information on where the whale was, what it was doing at the time, and what ocean conditions were like. Then, they can use all this information together to train AI systems to search for patterns that might reveal clues about what individual codas mean. "Most of what we've been doing so far has been focusing on the structure and the grammar of the language," he says. "We're trying to figure out, What are the words?"

They're also gathering even more data, David adds. The Project CETI team, which has grown to about thirty-five scientists, is designing new tracking devices that can record underwater videos and collect biological data, like heartbeat readings. One day, David hopes to be able to understand exactly what whales like Pinchy are communicating. But even if that never happens, learning more about these animals and challenging researchers to think beyond our own languages could yield information that's useful in lots of scientific disciplines, from marine biology and ecology to the fields of evolution and robotics. "We can't be tied to thinking like a human," he says.

WHEN WHALES USE THEIR STRONG TAIL FINS TO LAUNCH THEMSELVES OUT OF THE WATER, IT'S CALLED BREACHING.

ACTIVITY
CODED COMMUNIQUÉS

You don't need a whale to try your hand at code cracking. In this challenge, you and a partner will make a type of coded message called a book cipher that only you two will be able to understand.

YOU'LL NEED:

- a partner
- 2 writing utensils
- 2 pieces of paper
- 2 books (these can be any two books, including this one)

1. You and your partner each take a piece of paper, a writing utensil, and a book.

2. It's code-making time. Each of you flip through your books and pick out a word that you want to use in your secret message. For your first try at writing a code, choose a word that's in the main text of the book—stay away from words that are in pictures, diagrams, captions, or definition boxes.

3. When either of you finds a word you want to use, write it down, making sure to cover your paper with your hand so your partner can't see. Flip your paper over and write down three numbers:

- The first is the page number where the word is located.
- The second is the line number—count the lines starting at the top of the page, and when you get to the one with your word on it, that's your line number. Headlines count as a line, and if there's a chapter title or number at the very top of the page, that's also a line, so don't forget to count it.
- The third is the word number—starting from the left, count the words in the line until you reach yours. Words with dashes only count as one word.

4. Separate the page, line, and word numbers with dashes. It should look something like this: 117-3-3. That's the number code for the word *flip* on this page.

5. Repeat these steps for two more words. Your code could be three random words from this book, like *squirrels derby alien*, or you could pick three words from completely different chapters that make a funny sentence, like *Octopuses sleep nearby*. When you finish, your paper should have a three-number code for each word you chose.

6. When you're both ready, place your secret messages into your books, number side up, and swap books. Use your partner's book to try to decode their secret message. When you think you've got it, flip the page over to see if you were right.

Could you and your partner figure out what the other was trying to say? Spies throughout history have used book ciphers like this to relay secret messages. Because books and texts are common, everyday objects, spies could have them around and use them as code-cracking keys without arousing suspicion. Once you get a little practice writing book ciphers, you and your partner can send each other lots of secret messages. You can also hide coded notes in library books and leave them for each other to find.

Try a variation on this exercise by choosing one page of this book with your partner. Each of you think up a short secret message—just two words to start. Next, find a word on the page that starts with the first letter that your message starts with. Write down the line number, a dash, then the word number of that word starting from the left. Now, find that word that starts with the second letter of your message and write down the line and word number. Keep going until you've done all of the letters in the first word of your message. Then, write an *S* and encode the second word of your message. (If, for example, you were using this page to code the message *Oh, hi*, the code would look like this: 1-7 2-4 S 2-4 7-8.)

FOR FURTHER EXPLORATION

THIS BOOK IS JUST A TEENY-TINY introduction to the wide, wondrous world of brains and all the incredible things they do every single day. And as you know by now, there are so many more mysteries about the brain that scientists across the world are working to understand. Maybe you'll help solve them one day.

If you're interested in learning more about subjects in this book, here's a list of kid-friendly resources to get you started.

General Resources

Chudler, Eric H. "Neuroscience for Kids." https://faculty.washington.edu/chudler/neurok.html.

Couch, Christina, and Cara Giaimo. *Detector Dogs, Dynamite Dolphins, and More Animals with Super Sensory Powers*. Somerville: MIT Kids Press, 2022.

Dingman, Marc. "2-Minute Neuroscience." YouTube, https://www.youtube.com/playlist ?list=PLNZqyJnsvdMqFNFyHvMFrFnlXLosnwwB_.

How the Brain Works. New York: Penguin Random House, 2020.

"Life / Animals" and "Life / Brain" sections of *Science News Explores*, https://www.snexplores .org/topic/animals and https://www.snexplores.org/topic/brain.

National Geographic Readers. Book series. Washington, DC: National Geographic Books.

Scientists in the Field. Book series. Boston: Houghton Mifflin Harcourt.

Chapter 1: Innovative Octopuses

All About Octopuses

Drimmer, Stephanie Warren. *National Geographic Readers: Ink! 100 Fun Facts About Octopuses, Squid, and More*. Washington, DC: National Geographic Books, 2019.

Montgomery, Sy. *The Octopus Scientists: Exploring the Mind of a Mollusk*. Boston: HMH Books for Young Readers, 2015.

"Octopus." *NationalGeographicKids*.https://kids.nationalgeographic.com/animals/invertebrates/facts/octopus.

The Shedd Aquarium and Creatures Who Live There

"Animals." Shedd Aquarium. https://www.sheddaquarium.org/animals.

Cell Communication in Your Brain

Chudler, Eric H. "Cells of the Nervous System." *Neuroscience for Kids*, https://faculty.washington.edu/chudler/cells.html.

Ludwig, Mike. "How Your Brain Cells Talk to Each Other—Whispered Secrets and Public Announcements." *Frontiers for Young Minds*, July 26, 2017. https://kids.frontiersin.org/articles/10.3389/frym.2017.00039.

St. Clair, Bryn. "Explainer: What Is a Neuron?" *Science News Explores*, April 22, 2021. https://www.snexplores.org/article/explainer-what-is-a-neuron.

The Gut-Brain Axis

Brookshire, Bethany. "Belly Bacteria Can Shape Mood and Behavior." *Science News Explores*, June 7, 2018. https://www.snexplores.org/article/belly-bacteria-can-shape-mood-and-behavior.

Temming, Maria. "How Bugs in Your Gut Might Hijack Your Emotions." *Science News Explores*, October 16, 2017. https://www.snexplores.org/article/how-bugs-your-gut-might-hijack-your-emotions.

Octopus Brains

Short, Tal, and Nir Nesher. "The Octopus: A Unique Animal for Studying the Brain." *Frontiers for Young Minds*, November 23, 2021. https://kids.frontiersin.org/articles/10.3389/frym.2021.752743.

Wilke, Carolyn. "Analyze This: Octopuses May Use Favorite Arms for Grabbing Meals." *Science News Explores*, October 28, 2022. https://www.snexplores.org/article/analyze-this-octopuses-may-use-favorite-arms-for-grabbing-meals.

Octopus Antics and Abilities

Corpuz, Mina. "New England Aquarium Has Its Own Octopus Escape Story." *Boston Globe*, April 14, 2016. https://www.bostonglobe.com/metro/2016/04/14/new-england-aquarium-has-its-own-octopus-escape-story/3ShjEIp3tdIAqbLGPLtuSO/story.html.

Lambert, Jonathan. "Touching Allows Octopuses to Pre-Taste Their Food." *Science News Explores*, January 4, 2021. https://www.snexplores.org/article/octopus-touch-arms-suckers-taste-food.

Montgomery, Sy. *Inky's Amazing Escape: How a Very Smart Octopus Found His Way Home*. New York: Simon & Schuster / Paula Wiseman Books, 2018.

Astrobiology

"Learning Materials." Astrobiology at NASA. https://astrobiology.nasa.gov/classroom-materials/.

Chapter 2: Panic-Busting Parrots

Serenity Park's Parrots and Projects

"Parrot C.A.R.E. / Serenity Park." Lockwood Animal Rescue Center, https://lockwoodarc.org/serenity-park.

Fear and Stress in Your Brain and Body

Brookshire, Bethany. "Ow! These Cells Might Help Brains Remember Pain and Fear." *Science News Explores*, January 2, 2018. https://www.snexplores.org/article/ow-these-cells-might-help-brains-remember-pain-and-fear.

Chudler, Eric H. "Explore the Nervous System." Neuroscience for Kids, https://faculty.washington.edu/chudler/nsdivide.html.

Javanbakht, Arash, and Linda Saab. "The Science of Fright: Why We Love to be Scared." *The Conversation*, October 26, 2017. https://theconversation.com/the-science-of-fright-why-we-love-to-be-scared-85885.

Therapy Animals

Hurt, Avery Elizabeth. "In an Emergency, You May Want to See Dr. Dog." *Science News Explores*, April 13, 2022. https://www.snexplores.org/article/therapy-dog-reduces-pain-anxiety-emergency-room.

Meditation

Isbel, Ben. "A Gym Workout for Your Brain: How Mindfulness Can Help Improve Mental Health." *Frontiers for Young Minds*, March 1, 2019. https://kids.frontiersin.org/articles/10.3389/frym.2019.00034.

Chapter 3: Savvy Squirrels

Squirrel School Research and WildCare

Lambert, Jonathan. "Squirrels Use Parkour Tricks to Leap from Branch to Branch." *Science News Explores*, September 13, 2021. https://www.snexplores.org/article/squirrels-use-parkour-tricks-to-leap-from-branch-to-branch.

"A Squirrel's Guide to Success." *Nature*, directed by Tom Jarvis and Rowan Crawford, 2018.

"WildCare." WildCare, https://discoverwildcare.org.

Memory in Humans

"How Does Your Memory Work? | Head Squeeze." YouTube, BBC Earth Lab. https://youtu.be/TUoJc0NPajQ.

Kean, Sam. "What Happens When You Remove the Hippocampus?" TedEd, https://ed.ted.com/lessons/what-happens-when-you-remove-the-hippocampus-sam-kean.

Stevens, Alison Pearce. "Learning Rewires the Brain." *Science News Explores*, September 2, 2014. https://www.snexplores.org/article/learning-rewires-brain.

Animal Memory

Gendler, Alex. "Why Elephants Never Forget." YouTube, TedEd, https://www.youtube.com/watch?v=lSXNqsOoURg.

"Three Animals with Incredible Memories." *BBC Bitesiz*e, https://www.bbc.co.uk/bitesize/articles/zdkrvwx.

False Memories

Ornes, Stephen. "Fake Memories." *Science News Explores*, August 7, 2013. https://www.snexplores.org/article/fake-memories.

Schacter, Dan. "Are All of Your Memories Real?" TedEd, https://ed.ted.com/lessons/are-all-of-your-memories-real-daniel-l-schacter.

Chapter 4: Half-Brained Birds

Hawaii's Incredible Birds

"Birds Hawai'i Past Present." Birds Hawai'i Past Present, https://www.birdshawaiipastpresent .com.

"Kaua'i Forest Bird Recovery Project." Kaua'i Forest Bird Recovery Project, https://kauaiforestbirds.org.

Animals' Snoozing Brains

Bower, Bruce. "Compared to Other Primates, Humans Get Little Sleep." *Science News Explores*, April 9, 2018. https://www.snexplores.org/article/compared-other-primates -humans-get-little-sleep.

Faherty, Sheena. "How Does Hibernation Work?" TedEd, https://ed.ted.com/lessons /what-s-the-difference-between-hibernation-and-sleep-sheena-faherty.

"How the Animal Kingdom Sleeps." YouTube, *The Atlantic*, https://www.youtube.com /watch?v=A-JtybJbVbA.

Quintanilla, Mariah. "Surprise! Some Jellyfish Appear to Need Their zzz's." *Science News Explores*, November 13, 2017. https://www.snexplores.org/article/surprise-some -jellyfish-appear-need-their-zzzs.

Your Snoozing Brain

"BrainWorks: Sleep and the Brain." YouTube, UW Video channel. https://youtu.be /jR_t3gdSzrw.

Ornes, Stephen. "Sleeping Brains Take a Bath." *Science News Explores*, November 9, 2013. https://www.snexplores.org/article/sleeping-brains-take-bath.

Tamaki, Masako. "Can You Be Awake and Asleep at the Same Time?" YouTube, TedEd. https://www.ted.com/talks/masako_tamaki_can_you_be_awake_and_asleep_at_the _same_time/transcript?language=en.

Temming, Maria. "Let's Learn About Sleep." *Science News Explores*, May 31, 2022. https://www.snexplores.org/article/lets-learn-about-sleep.

Chapter 5: Timeless Tortoises

Jonathan, Saint Helena, and Gretchen Johnson

"An Introduction to The World's Oldest Land Inhabitant—Jonathan the Tortoise." YouTube, Green Renaissance. https://www.youtube.com/watch?v=UK3TvZQJKIg.

"Explorer Classroom | The Hidden History of St. Helena Island with Gretchen Johnson." YouTube, National Geographic Education. https://www.youtube.com/watch?v=dagjgXSYHSs.

Amazing Ways That Animals Age

Baggaley, Kate. "A Whale of a Lifespan." *Science News Explores*, January 20, 2015. https://www.snexplores.org/article/whale-lifespan.

Gammon, Katharine. "How Hydra Regrow Their Heads." *Discover Magazine*, December 10, 2021. https://www.discovermagazine.com/the-sciences/how-hydra-regrow-their-heads.

Osterloff, Emily. "Immortal Jellyfish: The Secret to Cheating Death." The Natural History Museum, https://www.nhm.ac.uk/discover/immortal-jellyfish-secret-to-cheating-death.html.

Genes and Aging in Your Body

"Is Height Genetic?" YouTube, Be Smart. https://www.youtube.com/watch?v=0cuO5OSDMbw.

Menesini, Monica. "Why Do Our Bodies Age?" TedEd, https://ed.ted.com/lessons/why-do-our-bodies-age-monica-menesini.

"What Is a Gene?" *KidsHealth*, https://kidshealth.org/en/kids/what-is-gene.html.

Chapter 6: Chatty Cetaceans

Project CETI and the Dominica Sperm Whale Project

"The Dominica Sperm Whale Project." The Dominica Sperm Whale Project, http://www.thespermwhaleproject.org.

Droesser, Christoph. "Are We on the Verge of Chatting with Whales?" *Hakai Magazine*, October 26, 2021. https://hakaimagazine.com/features/are-we-on-the-verge-of-chatting-with-whales.

"Explorer Classroom in the Field | Shane Gero: Whales in Dominica." YouTube, National Geographic Education. https://www.youtube.com/watch?v=fCUt40wPaig.

"Project CETI." Project CETI, https://www.projectceti.org.

Animal Communication

Andrus, Aubre, and Gabby Wild. *How to Speak Animal.* Washington, DC: National Geographic Kids, 2022.

Kennerson, Elliott. "How Elephants Listen . . . With Their Feet." *KQED*, July 17, 2018. https://www.kqed.org/science/1926248/how-elephants-listen-with-their-feet.

Human Language

Bell, Terena. "Computers Can Translate Languages, But First They Have to Learn." *Science News Explores*, November 30, 2017. https://www.snexplores.org/article/computers-can-translate-languages-first-they-have-learn.

"Brain Sides and New Language Learning." YouTube, One Minute Explorer. https://www.youtube.com/watch?v=0dj0at_mccI.

Futrell, Richard. "When Was Talking Invented? A Language Scientist Explains How This Unique Feature of Human Beings May Have Evolved." *The Conversation*, August 8, 2022. https://theconversation.com/when-was-talking-invented-a-language-scientist-explains-how-this-unique-feature-of-human-beings-may-have-evolved-186877.

SOURCE NOTES

Chapter 1: Innovative Octopuses

p. 2: "Sometimes she touches my arms . . . 'you did not taste good'": author interview with Zoë Hagberg.

p. 9: "Alien intelligence is probably not going to look human . . . a new path to intelligence": author interview with Dominic Sivitilli.

p. 10: "The brain makes all the big decisions . . . what to do to the arms": author interview with Jennifer Mather.

p. 11: "and that controls all the big stuff": ibid.

pp. 12–13: "When we're doing new projects . . . getting the lab results I want" and "When it comes to writing my lyrics . . . it's helped me to be a better artist": author interview with Ruby Ibarra.

p. 14: "It goes very fast . . . how you can improve": author interview with Anahí Espíndola.

p. 14: "As long as my feet . . . really happy person" and "like getting in a time machine . . . very useful skill for that": author interview with Elizabeth Sibert.

Chapter 2: Panic-Busting Parrots

p. 21: "The animals here are scared . . . That was the same way I was": author interview with Stan McDonald.

p. 24: "All of that is helping you . . . running away or fighting": author interview with Antonia Seligowski.

p. 28: "I was not going to open up to them": author interview with Stan McDonald.

p. 29: "By talking to the animals . . . taught me how to trust": ibid.

p. 31: "he automatically went on the attack": ibid.

p. 31: "Slowly, he realized . . . wasn't trying to fight back": author interview with Stan McDonald.

p. 31: "That was basically the turning point right there": ibid.

p. 32: "You're not the same person or the same animal that you were before experiencing it": author interview with Liana Zanette.

Chapter 3: Savvy Squirrels

p. 42: "and they're doing it really fast": author interview with Lucia Jacobs.

p. 43: "If something really embarrassing . . . never want this to happen again'" and "That's really what a memory is . . . all firing at the same time": author interview with Gina Poe.

p. 53: "Their brains literally get bigger when they're making these decisions": author interview with Lucia Jacobs.

Chapter 4: Half-Brained Birds

p. 62: "Birds are a very important . . . our everyday lives": author interview with Bret Nainoa Mossman.

p. 66: "It's when the heavy-duty cleanup gets done": author interview with Gina Poe.

p. 70: "they sleep when they can . . . day or night": author interview with Bret Nainoa Mossman.

p. 71: "a really big mystery" and "People sometimes write . . . are awaiting discoveries": author interview with Niels Rattenborg.

p. 73: "In the Hawaiian worldview . . . like tending to your family": author interview with Bret Nainoa Mossman.

Chapter 5: Timeless Tortoises

p. 80: "he doesn't really age in the way that we do": author interview with Joe Hollins.

p. 84: "absolutely no signs of aging" and "It's a very unusual case": author interview with Steve Austad.

p. 86: "I thought he was pretty much . . . starving to death": author interview with Joe Hollins.

pp. 89, 92: "Most people think . . . all of the variation in human longevity" and "probably about 99 percent": author interview with Steve Austad.

pp. 96, 97: "It's like this missing part . . . piece together the story" and "When I was first researching . . . There's so much to learn": author interview with Gretchen Johnson.

Chapter 6: Chatty Cetaceans

pp. 108–109: "One thing that makes the human brain unique . . . It's beyond any one sense": author interview with Rodrigo Braga.

pp. 114, 115: "We don't have correspondences between words in English and words in whale-ese" and "Most of what . . . What are the words?": author interview with Jacob Andreas.

p. 115: "We can't be tied to thinking like a human": author interview with David Gruber.

BIBLIOGRAPHY

Allen, Marek C., Michael Clinchy, and Liana Y. Zanette. "Fear of Predators in Free-Living Wildlife Reduces Population Growth over Generations." *PNAS* 119, no. 7 (2022): e2112404119. https://doi.org/10.1073/pnas.2112404119.

American Bird Conservancy. "Band-Rumped Storm-Petrel." Accessed May 25, 2022. https://abcbirds.org/bird/band-rumped-storm-petrel.

———. "Hawaii." Accessed May 25, 2022. https://abcbirds.org/program/hawaii/.

American Psychological Association. "Stress Effects on the Body." November 1, 2018. https://www.apa.org/topics/stress/body.

Anthes, Emily. "The Animal Translators." *New York Times*, August 30, 2022. https://www.nytimes.com/2022/08/30/science/translators-animals-naked-mole-rats.html.

Arnold, Carrie. "Rhinos Use Poop Piles Like a Social Network." *National Geographic*, January 10, 2017. https://www.nationalgeographic.com/animals/article/rhinoceroses-poop-middens-communication?loggedout=true.

Atwal, Sanj. "190-Year-Old Jonathan Becomes World's Oldest Tortoise Ever." Guinness World Records, January 12, 2022. https://www.guinnessworldrecords.com/news/2022/1/190-year-old-jonathan-becomes-worlds-oldest-tortoise-ever-688683.

Azevedo, Frederico A. C., et al. "Equal Numbers of Neuronal and Nonneuronal Cells Make the Human Brain an Isometrically Scaled-Up Primate Brain." *The Journal of Comparative Neurology* 513, issue 5 (2009): 532–541. https://doi.org/10.1002/cne.21974.

Baker, Beth. "Unusual Adaptations: Evolution of the Mimic Octopus." *BioScience* 60, no. 11 (2010): 962. https://doi.org/10.1525/bio.2010.60.11.18.

Bale, Rachael. "What Are the Biggest Animals Among Us?" *National Geographic*, January 2, 2020. https://www.nationalgeographic.com/newsletters/animals/article/what-biggest-animals-among-us-january-02.

Ball, Philip. "The Challenges of Animal Translation." *The New Yorker*, April 27, 2021. https://www.newyorker.com/science/elements/the-challenges-of-animal-translation.

Balter, Michael. "The Incredible Shrinking Human Brain." *Science*, July 25, 2011. https://www.science.org/content/article/incredible-shrinking-human-brain.

Barber, Elizabeth. "200-Year-Old Rockfish Caught Off Alaska Coast." *Christian Science Monitor*, July 3, 2013. https://www.csmonitor.com/Science/2013/0703/200-year-old-rockfish-caught-off-Alaska-coast.

Barrett, Lisa Feldman. *Seven and a Half Lessons About the Brain*. Boston: Houghton Mifflin Harcourt, 2020.

Basso, Julia C., Alexandra McHale, Victoria Ende, Douglas J. Oberlin, and Wendy A. Suzuki. "Brief, Daily Meditation Enhances Attention, Memory, Mood, and Emotional Regulation in Non-Experienced Meditators." *Behavioural Brain Research* 356 (2019): 208–220. https://doi.org/10.1016/j.bbr.2018.08.023.

Bilefsky, Dan. "Inky the Octopus Escapes from a New Zealand Aquarium." *New York Times*, April 13, 2016. https://www.nytimes.com/2016/04/14/world/asia/inky-octopus-new-zealand-aquarium.html.

Bruck, Jason N. "Decades-Long Social Memory in Bottlenose Dolphins." *Proceedings of the Royal Society B* 208, no. 1768 (2013): 20131726. https://doi.org/10.1098/rspb.2013.1726.

Brulliard, Karin. "Therapy Animals Are Everywhere. Proof That They Help Is Not." *The Washington Post*, July 2, 2017. https://www.washingtonpost.com/news/animalia/wp/2017/07/02/therapy-animals-are-everywhere-proof-that-they-help-is-not.

Callaway, Ewen. "What DNA Reveals about St. Helena's Freed Slaves." *Nature* 540 (2016): 184–187. https://doi.org/10.1038/540184a.

Camilleri, Michael. "Serotonin in the Gastrointestinal Tract." *Current Opinion in Endocrinology, Diabetes and Obesity* 16, no. 1 (2009): 53–59. https://doi.org/10.1097/med.0b013e32831e9c8e.

Cantor, Matthew. "'The Magic of Llamas': Furry Friends Help Stressed University Students Relax." *The Guardian*, May 4, 2019. https://www.theguardian.com/us-news/2019/may/04/llamapalooza-uc-berkeley-llama-stressed-student-mental-health.

Cantor, Maurício, Lauren G. Shoemaker, Reniel B. Cabral, César O. Flores, Melinda Varga, and Hal Whitehead. "Multilevel Animal Societies Can Emerge from Cultural Transmission." *Nature Communications* 6, 8091 (2015). https://doi.org/10.1038/ncomms9091.

Carabotti, Marilia., et al. "The Gut-Brain Axis: Interactions between Enteric Microbiota, Central and Enteric Nervous Systems." *Annals of Gastroenterology* 28, no. 2 (2015): 203–209.

Carey, Ben, et al. "Outcomes of a Controlled Trial with Visiting Therapy Dog Teams on Pain in Adults in an Emergency Department." *PLOS ONE* 17, no. 3 (2022): e0262599. https://doi.org/10.1371/journal.pone.0262599.

Carruthers, Peter. "Evolution of Working Memory." In *The Human Mental Machinery*, edited by C. J. Cela-Conde, R. Gutierrez Lombardo, J. C. Avise, et al., 10371–10378. Vol. 7 of *In the Light of Evolution*. Washington, DC: National Academies Press, 2014.

Cassella, Carly. "This New AI Can Detect the Calls of Animals Swimming in an Ocean of Noise." Science Alert, May 24, 2022. https://www.sciencealert.com/new-ai-tool-recognizes-animal-chatter-in-the-ocean-and-it-s-called-deepsqueak.

Cassill, Deby L., Skye Brown, Devon Swick, and George Yanev. "Polyphasic Wake/Sleep Episodes in the Fire Ant, *Solenopsis invicta*." *Journal of Insect Behavior* 22 (2009): 313–323. https://doi.org/10.1007/s10905-009-9173-4.

Cerchio, Salvatore, et al. "A New Blue Whale Song-Type Described for the Arabian Sea and Western Indian Ocean." *Endangered Species Research* 43 (2020): 495–515. https://doi.org/10.3354/esr01096.

Cherniack, E. Paul, and Ariella R. Cherniack. "The Benefit of Pets and Animal-Assisted Therapy to the Health of Older Individuals." *Current Gerontology and Geriatrics Research* 2014 (2014). https://doi.org/10.1155/2014/623203.

Chudler, Eric. H. "Brain Facts That Make You Go, 'Hmmmmm.'" Neuroscience for Kids. Accessed September 18, 2022. https://faculty.washington.edu/chudler/facts.html.

———. "Brain Facts and Figures." Neuroscience for Kids. Accessed September 18, 2022. https://faculty.washington.edu/chudler/facts.html.

Clinchy, Michael, Liana Zanette, Rudy Boonstra, John C. Wingfield, and James N. M. Smith. "Balancing Food and Predator Pressure Induces Chronic Stress in Songbirds." *Proceedings of the Royal Society B* 217, no. 1556 (2004): 2473–2479. https://doi.org/10.1098/rspb.2004.2913.

Clinchy, Michael, et al. "Fear of the Human 'Super Predator' Far Exceeds the Fear of Large Carnivores in a Model Mesocarnivore." *Behavioral Ecology* 27, no. 6 (2016): 1826–1832. https://doi.org/10.1093/beheco/arw117.

Colorado Department of Education. "Watermelon Information Sheet." Accessed September 22, 2022. https://www.cde.state.co.us/nutrition/osnffvpproduceinfosheetswatermelons.

Colten, H. R., and B. M. Altevogt, eds. *Sleep Disorders and Sleep Deprivation: An Unmet Public Health Problem*. Washington, DC: National Academies Press, 2006.

Crossman, Molly K. "Effects of Interactions with Animals on Human Psychological Distress." *Journal of Clinical Psychology* 73, no. 7 (2017): 761–784. https://doi.org/10.1002/jclp.22410.

Curtis, Deborah J., Alphonse Zaramody, and Robert D. Martin. "Cathemerality in the Mongoose Lemur, *Eulemur mongoz*." *American Journal of Primatology* 47, no. 4 (1999): 279–298. https://doi.org/10.1002/(SICI)1098-2345(1999)47:4<279: AID-AJP2>3.0.CO;2-U.

Dao, James. "After Duty, Dogs Suffer Like Soldiers." *New York Times*, December 1, 2011. https://www.nytimes.com/2011/12/02/us/more-military-dogs-show-signs-of-combat-stress.html.

Dave, A. S., and D. Margoliash. "Song Replay During Sleep and Computational Rules for Sensorimotor Vocal Learning." *Science* 290, no. 5492 (2000): 812–816. https://doi.org/10.1126/science.290.5492.812.

Delgado, Mikel, and Lucia Jacobs. "Caching for Where and What: Evidence for a Mnemonic Strategy in a Scatter-Hoarder." *Royal Society Open Science* 4, no. 9 (2017): 170958. https://doi.org/10.1098/rsos.170958.

Dixon, M. May, Patricia Jones, Michael Ryan, Gerald Carter, and Rachel Page. "Long-Term Memory in Frog-Eating Bats." *Current Biology* 32, no. 12 (2022): PR557–R558. https://doi.org/10.1016/j.cub.2022.05.031.

Duke Lemur Center. "Mongoose Lemur." Accessed December 1, 2022. https://lemur.duke.edu/discover/meet-the-lemurs/mongoose-lemur.

Encyclopaedia Britannica Online. "History of Hawaii." Accessed August 8, 2022. https://www.britannica.com/place/Hawaii-state/History.

———. "Saint Helena." Accessed October 2, 2022. https://www.britannica.com/place/Saint-Helena-island-South-Atlantic-Ocean.

Engelhardt, Elias. "Hippocampus Discovery First Steps." *Dementia and Neuropsychologia* 10, no. 1 (2016): 58–62. https://doi.org/10.1590/S1980-57642016DN10100011.

Ferrari, Robert, Gianluca Campo, Elisa Gardini, Giovanni Pasanisi, and Claudio Ceconi. "Specific and Selective I_f Inhibition: Expected Clinical Benefits from Pure Heart Rate Reduction in Coronary Patients." *European Heart Journal Supplements* 7, suppl_H (2005): H16–H21. https://doi.org/10.1093/eurheartj/sui048.

Finn, Julian K., Tim Tregenza, and Mark D. Norman. "Defensive Tool Use in a Coconut-Carrying Octopus." *Current Biology* 19, no. 23 (2009): R1069–R1070. https://doi.org/10.1016/j.cub.2009.10.052.

Florida Museum of Natural History. "*Carcharhinus amblyrhynchos*." Accessed October 3, 2022. https://www.floridamuseum.ufl.edu/discover-fish/species-profiles/carcharhinus-amblyrhynchos.

Foley, Charles, Nathalie Pettorelli, and Lara Foley. "Severe Drought and Calf Survival in Elephants." *Biology Letters* 4 (2008): 541–544. https://doi.org/10.1098/rsbl.2008.0370.

Fox, Kieran C. R., Michael Muthukrishna, and Susanne Shultz. "The Social and Cultural Roots of Whale and Dolphin Brains." *Nature Ecology & Evolution* 1 (2017): 1699–1705. https://doi.org/10.1038/s41559-017-0336-y.

Frank, Marcos G., Robert H. Waldrop, Michelle Dumoulin, Sara Aton, and Jean G. Boal. "A Preliminary Analysis of Sleep-Like States in the Cuttlefish *Sepia officinalis*." *PLOS ONE* 7, no. 6 (2012): e38125. https://doi.org/10.1371/journal.pone.0038125.

Furness, John B., Brid P. Callaghan, Leni R. Rivera, and Hyun-Jung Cho. "The Enteric Nervous System and Gastrointestinal Innervation: Integrated Local and Central Control." In *Microbial Endocrinology: The Microbiota-Gut-Brain Axis in Health and Disease*, edited by M. Lyte and J. Cryan, 39–71. New York: Springer, 2014.

George, Alison. *The Brain: A User's Guide*. New York: Nicholas Brealey Publishing, 2018.

Gero, Shane, Hal Whitehead, and Luke Rendell. "Individual, Unit and Vocal Clan Level Identity Cues in Sperm Whale Codas." *Royal Society Open Science* 3, no. 1 (2016): 150372. https://doi.org/10.1098/rsos.150372.

Gero, Shane, Anne Bøttcher, Hal Whitehead, and Peter Teglberg Madsen. "Socially Segregated, Sympatric Sperm Whale Clans in the Atlantic Ocean." *Royal Society Open Science* 3, no. 6 (2016): 160061. https://doi.org/10.1098/rsos.160061.

Ghirlanda, Stefano, Johan Lind, and Magnus Enquist. "Memory for Stimulus Sequences: A Divide Between Humans and Other Animals?" *Royal Society Open Science* 4, no. 6 (2017): 161011. https://doi.org/10.1098/rsos.161011.

Givon, Shachar, Matan Samina, Ohad Ben-Shahar, and Ronen Segev. "From Fish Out Of Water to New Insights on Navigation Mechanisms in Animals." *Behavioural Brain Research* 419 (2022): 113711. doi.org/10.1016/j.bbr.2021.113711.

Gong, Zhiwen, Ken Tan, and James C. Niehl. "Hornets Possess Long-Lasting Olfactory Memories." *Journal of Experimental Biology* 222, no. 13 (2019): jeb200881. https://doi.org/10.1242/jeb.200881.

Hadj-Chikh, Leila Z., Michael A. Steele, and Peter D. Smallwood. "Caching Decisions by Grey Squirrels: A Test of the Handling Time and Perishability Hypotheses." *Animal Behaviour* 52, no. 5 (1996): 941–948. https://doi.org/10.1006/anbe.1996.0242.

Hague, Theresa, Michaela Florini, and Paul L. R. Andrews. "Preliminary in Vitro Functional Evidence for Reflex Responses to Noxious Stimuli in the Arms of *Octopus vulgaris*." *Journal of Experimental Marine Biology and Ecology* 447 (2013): 100–105. https://doi.org/10.1016/j.jembe.2013.02.016.

Harmon, Katherine. "How Did a Giant Octopus Lose the Battle of Seattle?" *Scientific American*, October 21, 2013. https://blogs.scientificamerican.com/octopus-chronicles/how-did-a-giant-octopus-lose-the-battle-of-seattle.

Hart, Benjamin L., Lynette A. Hart, and Noa Pinter-Wollman. "Large Brains and Cognition: Where Do Elephants Fit In?" *Neuroscience & Biobehavioral Reviews* 32, no. 1 (2008): 86–98. https://doi.org/10.1016/j.neubiorev.2007.05.012.

Hawaiian Government Division of State Parks. "Wildlife." Accessed August 5, 2022. https://dlnr.hawaii.gov/dsp/wildlife.

Helms, Christine. "NASCAR May Be the Fastest Way to Learn About Physics." *The Conversation*, August 8, 2019. https://theconversation.com/nascar-may-be-the-fastest-way-to-learn-about-physics-118641.

Hersh, Taylor A., et al. "Evidence from Sperm Whale Clans of Symbolic Marking in Non-Human Cultures." *PNAS* 119, no. 37 (2022): E2201692119. https://doi.org/10.1073/pnas.2201692119.

Hess, Steven C., and Paul C. Banko. "Feral Cats: Too Long a Threat to Hawaiian Wildlife." *Publications of the US Geological Survey*, 2006. https://digitalcommons.unl.edu/cgi/viewcontent.cgi?article=1111&context=usgspubs.

Hunt, Nathaniel H., Judy Jinn, Lucia Jacobs, and Robert Full. "Acrobatic Squirrels Learn to Leap and Land on Tree Branches Without Falling." *Science* 373, no. 6555 (2021): 697–700. https://doi.org10.1126/science.abe5753.

Ichitani, Tatiane, and Maria Claudia Cunha. "Effects of Animal-Assisted Activity on Self-Reported Feelings of Pain in Hospitalized Children and Adolescents." *Psicologia: Reflexão e Crítica* 29, 43 (2016). https://doi.org/10.1186/s41155-016-0049-1.

Institute for Quality and Efficiency in Health Care. "How Does the Brain Work?" Informedhealth.org. Last modified October 31, 2018. https://www.ncbi.nlm.nih.gov/books/NBK279302/#:~:text=The%20human%20brain%20is%20roughly,cells%20which%20stabilize%20the%20tissue.

Jacobs, Lucia F., and Emily R. Liman. "Grey Squirrels Remember the Locations of Buried Nuts." *Animal Behavior* 41, no. 1 (1991): 103–110. https://doi.org/10.1016/S0003-3472(05)80506-8.

Jochum, K. P., et al. "Whole-Ocean Changes in Silica and Ge/Si Ratios During the Last Deglacial Deduced from Long-Lived Giant Glass Sponges." *Geophysical Research Letters* 44, no. 22 (2017): 11555–11564. https://doi.org/10.1002/2017GL073897.

Jones, Owen R., et al. "Diversity of Ageing across the Tree of Life." *Nature* 505 (2014): 169–173. https://doi.org/10.1038/nature12789.

Kannan, Madhuvanthi. "Chimps Outplay Humans in Brain Games." *Scientific American,* September 2, 2014. https://www.scientificamerican.com/article/chimps-outplay-humans-in-brain-games1.

Katsuki, Takeo, and Ralph J. Greenspan. "Jellyfish Nervous Systems." *Current Biology* 23, no. 14 (2013): PR592–R594. https://doi.org/10.1016/j.cub.2013.03.057.

Keene, Alex C., and Erik R. Duboue. "The Origins and Evolution of Sleep." *Journal of Experimental Biology* 221, no. 11 (2018): jeb159533. https://doi.org/10.1242/jeb.159533.

Kershenbaum, Arik, et al. "Disentangling Canid Howls across Multiple Species and Subspecies: Structure in a Complex Communication Channel." *Behavioural Processes* 124 (2016): 149–157. https://doi.org/10.1016/j.beproc.2016.01.006.

Khoury, Bassam, et al. "Mindfulness-Based Therapy: A Comprehensive Meta-Analysis." *Clinical Psychology Review* 33, no. 6 (2013): 763–771. https://doi.org/10.1016/j.cpr.2013.05.005.

Kleist, Nathan J., Robert P. Guralnick, Alexander Cruz, and Christopher A. Lowry. "Chronic Anthropogenic Noise Disrupts Glucocorticoid Signaling and Has Multiple Effects on Fitness in an Avian Community." *PNAS* 115, no. 4 (2018): E648–E657. https://doi.org/10.1073/pnas.1709200115.

Kumar, Ruchi. "Can Animals Suffer from PTSD?" *Washington Post*, July 8, 2017. https://www.washingtonpost.com/news/animalia/wp/2017/07/08/can-animals-suffer-from-ptsd.

Kverková, Kristina, Alexandra Polonyiová, Lukáš Kubička, and Pavel Němec. "Individual and Age-Related Variation of Cellular Brain Composition in a Squamate Reptile." *Biology Letters* 16, no. 9 (2020): 20200280. https://doi.org/10.1098/rsbl.2020.0280.

Lameira, Adriano R., and Josep Call. "Time-Space–Displaced Responses in the Orangutan Vocal System." *Science Advances* 4, no. 11 (2018). https://doi.org/10.1126/sciadv .aau3401.

Langley, Liz. "Do Animals Dream?" *National Geographic*, September 5, 2015. https://www .nationalgeographic.com/culture/article/150905-animals-sleep-science-dreaming -cats-brains?loggedin=true&rnd=1668708214384.

Larson, Samantha. "Oldest Clam Consternation Overblown." *National Geographic*, November 17, 2013. https://www.nationalgeographic.com/animals/article/131116 -oldest-clam-dead-ming-science-ocean-507.

Laskow, Sarah. "A 10-Foot Long, 11,000-Year-Old Sponge Skeleton Has a Hidden Use." *Atlas Obscura*, March 1, 2018. https://www.atlasobscura.com/articles/sponge -record-climate-change-data.

Louie, Kenway, and Matthew A. White. "Temporally Structured Replay of Awake Hippocampal Ensemble Activity during Rapid Eye Movement Sleep." *Neuron* 29, no. 1 (2001): 145–156. https://doi.org/10.1016/S0896-6273(01)00186-6.

Manoach, Dara S., and Robert Strickgold. "Sleep: Keeping One Eye Open." *Current Biology* 26, no. 9 (2016): R360–R361. https://doi.org/10.1016/j.cub.2016.03.041.

Marneweck, Courtney, Andreas Jürgens, and Adrian M. Shrader. "Dung Odours Signal Sex, Age, Territorial and Oestrous State in White Rhinos." *Proceedings of the Royal Society B* 284, no. 1846 (2017): 20162376. https://doi.org/10.1098/rspb.2016.2376.

Martin, Christopher Flynn, Rahul Bhui, Peter Bossaerts, Tetsuro Matsuzawa, and Colin Camerer. "Chimpanzee Choice Rates in Competitive Games Match Equilibrium Game Theory Predictions." *Scientific Reports* 4, 5182 (2014). https://doi.org/10.1038/srep05182.

Mayne, Benjamin, Oliver Berry, Campbell Davies, Jessica Farley, and Simon Jarman. "A Genomic Predictor of Lifespan in Vertebrates." *Scientific Reports* 9, 17866 (2019). https:// doi.org/10.1038/s41598-019-54447-w.

McMurray, S. E., J. E. Blum, and J. R. Pawlik. "Redwood of the Reef: Growth and Age of the Giant Barrel Sponge *Xestospongia muta* in the Florida Keys." *Marine Biology* 155 (2008): 159–171. https://doi.org/10.1007/s00227-008-1014-z.

Medeiros, Sylvia Lima de Souza, et al. "Cyclic Alternation of Quiet and Active Sleep States in the Octopus." *iScience* 24, no. 4 (2021): 102223. https://doi.org/10.1016/j.isci.2021.102223.

Miller, Greg. "How Our Brains Make Memories." *Smithsonian Magazine*, May 2010. https://www .smithsonianmag.com/science-nature/how-our-brains-make-memories-14466850/.

Mortimer, Beth, William Rees, Paula Koelemeijer, and Tarje Nissen-Meyer. "Classifying Elephant Behaviour through Seismic Vibrations." *Current Biology* 28, no. 9 (2018): PR547– R548. https://doi.org/10.1016/j.cub.2018.03.062.

Mubanga, Mwenya, et al. "Dog Ownership and the Risk of Cardiovascular Disease and Death—A Nationwide Cohort Study." *Scientific Reports* 7, 15821 (2017). https://doi.org /10.1038/s41598-017-16118-6.

NASA. "Orion Service Module Testing Sounds Off." May 25, 2016. https://www.nasa.gov /feature/orion-service-module-testing-sounds-off.

Nath, Ravi D., et al. "The Jellyfish *Cassiopea* Exhibits a Sleep-like State." *Current Biology* 27, no. 19 (2017): P2984–2990.E3. https://doi.org/10.1016/j.cub.2017.08.014.

National Geographic. "Photo Ark." Accessed September 1, 2022. https://www.nationalgeographic.org/projects/photo-ark.

National Human Genome Research Institute. "Human Genome Project." Accessed October 2, 2022. https://www.genome.gov/about-genomics/educational-resources/fact-sheets/human-genome-project.

National Institute of Mental Health. "Post-Traumatic Stress Disorder." Accessed March 3, 2022. https://www.nimh.nih.gov/health/topics/post-traumatic-stress-disorder-ptsd.

National Oceanic and Atmospheric Administration. "How Long Do Greenland Sharks Live?" Accessed October 14, 2022. https://oceanservice.noaa.gov/facts/greenland-shark.html.

———. "Scientists Discover Largest Sponge Known During Deep-Sea Exploration." May 25, 2016. https://www.noaa.gov/news/scientists-discover-largest-sponge-known-during-deep-sea-exploration.

Nealon, Lizzie. "Average Car Weight." Bankrate.com, October 20, 2021. https://www.bankrate.com/insurance/car/average-car-weight.

New Zealand Government Department of Conservation. "Tuatara." Accessed October 29, 2022. https://www.doc.govt.nz/nature/native-animals/reptiles-and-frogs/tuatara.

Nielsen, Jared A., Brandon A. Zielinski, Michael A. Ferguson, Janet E. Lainhart, and Jeffrey S. Anderson. "An Evaluation of the Left-Brain vs. Right-Brain Hypothesis with Resting State Functional Connectivity Magnetic Resonance Imaging." *PLOS ONE* 8 (2013): e71275. https://doi.org/10.1371/journal.pone.0071275.

NOAA Fisheries. "Scalloped Hammerhead Shark." Accessed April 15, 2022. https://www.fisheries.noaa.gov/species/scalloped-hammerhead-shark.

———. "Species Directory." Accessed October 26, 2022. https://www.fisheries.noaa.gov/species-directory.

Nunes, Ashley, and Arthur F. Kramer. "Experienced-Based Mitigation of Age-Related Performance Declines: Evidence from Air Traffic Control." *Journal of Experimental Psychology: Applied* 15, no. 1 (2009). https://doi.org/10.1037/a0014947.

Orlando, Alex. "Why Do We Dream? Science Offers a Few Possibilities." *Discover Magazine*, December 10, 2020. https://www.discovermagazine.com/mind/why-do-we-dream-science-offers-a-few-possibilities.

Pagel, Mark. "Q&A: What Is Human Language, When Did It Evolve and Why Should We Care?" *BMC Biology* 15 (2017): 64. https://doi.org/10.1186/s12915-017-0405-3.

Pascual-Turner, Maria, et al. "Comparative Genomics of Mortal and Immortal Cnidarians Unveils Novel Keys Behind Rejuvenation." *PNAS* 119, no. 36 (2022): e2118763119. https://doi.org/10.1073/pnas.2118763119.

Pearson, Andrew. "Dataset to Accompany the Excavation Report for a 'Liberated African' Graveyard in Rupert's Valley, St. Helena, South Atlantic." *Journal of Open Archaeology Data* 1 (2012): e5. https://doi.org/10.5334/4f7b093ed0a77.

Pearson, Andrew. "Infernal Traffic: Excavation of a Liberated African Graveyard in Rupert's Valley, St. Helena." Archaeology Data Service (2012). https://doi.org/10.5284/1011174.

Peiser, Jaclyn. "A Squirrel Hid Thousands of Walnuts Under the Hood of a Man's Truck. It Wasn't the First Time." *The Washington Post*, September 30, 2021. https://www.washingtonpost.com/nation/2021/09/30/squirrel-truck-fargo-bill-fischer.

Pendry, Patricia, and Jaymie L. Vandagriff. "Animal Visitation Program (AVP) Reduces Cortisol Levels of University Students: A Randomized Controlled Trial." *AERA Open* 5, no. 2 (2019). https://doi.org/10.1177/2332858419852592.

Pennisi, Elizabeth. "Meet the Psychobiome." *Science* 368, no. 6491 (2020): 570–573. https://doi.org/10.1126/science.368.6491.570.

Piriano, S., F. Boero, B. Aeschbach, and V. Schmid. "Reversing the Life Cycle: Medusae Transforming into Polyps and Cell Transdifferentiation in *Turritopsis nutricula*." *The Biological Bulletin* 190, no. 3 (1996). https://doi.org/10.2307/1543022.

Pool, Bob. "Did This Mollusk Open a Bivalve?" *Los Angeles Times*, February 27, 2009. https://www.latimes.com/archives/la-xpm-2009-feb-27-me-octopus27-story.html.

Prat, Yosef, Lindsay Azoulay, Roi Dor, and Yossi Yovel. "Crowd Vocal Learning Induces Vocal Dialects in Bats: Playback of Conspecifics Shapes Fundamental Frequency Usage by Pups." *PloS Biology* 15, no. 10 (2017): e2002556. https://doi.org/10.1371/journal.pbio.2002556.

Queensland Government Department of Environment and Science. "Koala Facts." Accessed April 13, 2022. https://environment.des.qld.gov.au/wildlife/animals/living-with/koalas/facts.

Quesada, Victor, et al. "Giant Tortoise Genomes Provide Insights into Longevity and Age-Related Disease." *Nature Ecology and Evolution* 3 (2019): 87–95. https://doi.org/10.1038/s41559-018-0733-x.

Rattenborg, Niels C. "Sleeping on the Wing." *Interface Focus* 7, no. 1 (2017). https://doi.org/10.1098/rsfs.2016.0082.

Rattenborg, Niels C., Steven L. Lima, and Charles J. Amlaner. "Half-Awake to the Risk of Predation." *Nature* 397 (1999): 397–398. https://doi.org/10.1038/17037.

Rattenborg, Niels C., et al. "Evidence That Birds Sleep in Mid-Flight." *Nature Communications* 7, 12468 (2016): 12468. https://doi.org/10.1038/ncomms12468.

Rendell, L. E., and H. Whitehead. "Vocal Clans in Sperm Whales (*Physeter macrocephalus*)." *Proceedings of the Royal Society B* 270, no. 1512 (2003): 225–231. https://doi.org/10.1098/rspb.2002.2239.

Richter, Jonas N., Binyamin Hochner, and Michael J. Kuba. "Pull or Push? Octopuses Solve a Puzzle Problem." *PLOS ONE* 11 (2016): e0152048. https://doi.org/10.1371/journal.pone.0152048.

Ritchie, James. "Fact or Fiction? Elephants Never Forget." *Scientific American*, January 12, 2009. https://www.scientificamerican.com/article/elephants-never-forget/?gclid=Cj0KCQjwnvOaBhDTARIsAJf8eVMCVwsBtPZRaRFMb0JlkQWHdRr10hPk3HJIAJK6Fp33n5AXexuBdvMaAqZeEALw_wcB.

Roach, Sean P., and Leslie S. Phillmore. "Geographic Variation in Song Structure in the Hermit Thrush." *The Auk* 134, no. 3 (2017): 612–626. https://doi.org/10.1642/AUK-16-222.1.

Rodrigo-Claverol, Maylos, Carles Casanova-Gonzalvo, Belén Malla-Clua, Esther Rodrigo-Claverol, Júlia Jové-Naval, and Marta Ortega-Bravo. "Animal-Assisted Intervention Improves Pain Perception in Polymedicated Geriatric Patients with Chronic Joint Pain: A Clinical Trial." *International Journal of Environmental Research and Public Health* 16, no. 16 (2019): 2843. doi.org/10.3390/ijerph16162843.

Rodriguez, Fernando, Emilio Duran, Juan Vargas, Blas Torres, and Cosme Salas. "Performance of Goldfish Trained in Allocentric and Egocentric Maze Procedures Suggests the Presence of a Cognitive Mapping System in Fishes." *Animal Learning and Behavior* 22 (1994): 409–420. https://doi.org/10.3758/BF03209160.

Romero-Mujalli, Daniel, Tjard Bergmann, Axel Zimmermann, and Marina Scheumann. "Utilizing DeepSqueak for Automatic Detection and Classification of Mammalian Vocalizations: A Case Study on Primate Vocalizations." *Scientific Reports* 11, 24463 (2021). https://doi.org/10.1038/s41598-021-03941-1.

Rosza, Matthew. "Chimpanzees Have Their Own Language—and Scientists Just Learned How They Put 'Words' Together." *Salon.com*, May 22, 2022. https://www.salon.com/2022/05/22/chimpanzees-have-their-own-language--and-scientists-just-learned-how-they-put-words-together.

San Francisco International Airport. "Meet the Wag Brigade." Accessed April 15, 2022. https://www.flysfo.com/passengers/services-amenities/wag-brigade.

Seay, Tina Hesman. "Both Fish and Humans Have REM-like Sleep." *Science News*, July 10, 2019. https://www.sciencenews.org/article/both-fish-and-humans-have-rem-sleep#:~:text=As%2520the%2520zebrafish%2520prepares%2520for,eye%2520movement%2520sleep%2520in%2520mammals.

Sherry, David F., Lucia F. Jacobs, and Steven J. C. Gaulin. "Spatial Memory and Adaptive Specialization of the Hippocampus." *Trends in Neurosciences* 15, no. 8 (1992): 298–303.

Shupak, Amanda. "The Peacock Spider's Adorable Dance Moves Will Captivate You." *CBS News*, August 3, 2015. https://www.cbsnews.com/news/the-peacock-spiders-adorable-dance-will-captivate-you.

Siebert, Charles. "What Does a Parrot Know About PTSD." *New York Times*, January 28, 2016. https://www.nytimes.com/2016/01/31/magazine/what-does-a-parrot-know-about-ptsd.html.

Sonntag, Mandy, and Thomas Arendt. "Neuronal Activity in the Hibernating Brain." *Frontiers in Neuroanatomy* 13 (2019). https://doi.org/10.3389/fnana.2019.00071.

Subbaraman, Nidhi. "'Octopus!': Eight Legs, One Brain and Plenty of Smarts." *NBC News*, October 30, 2013. https://www.nbcnews.com/sciencemain/octopus-eight-legs-one-brain-plenty-smarts-8c11490342.

Sumbre, German, Yoram Gutfreund, Graziano Fiorito, Tamar Flash, and Binyamin Hochner. "Control of Octopus Arm Extension by a Peripheral Motor Program." *Science* 293, no. 5536 (2001): 1845–1848. https://doi.org/10.1126/science.1060976.

Suraci, Justin P., Michael Clinchy, Lawrence M. Dill, Devin Roberts, and Liana Y. Zanette. "Fear of Large Carnivores Causes a Trophic Cascade." *Nature Communications* 7, 10698 (2016). https://www.nature.com/articles/ncomms10698.

Suzuki, Toshitaka N., David Wheatcroft, and Michael Griesser. "Experimental Evidence for Compositional Syntax in Bird Calls." *Nature Communications* 7, 10986 (2016). https://doi.org/10.1038/ncomms10986.

Tamaki, Masako, Ji Won Bang, Takeo Watanabe, and Yuka Sasaki. "Night Watch in One Brain Hemisphere during Sleep Associated with the First-Night Effect in Humans." *Current Biology* 26, no. 9 (2016): 1190–1194. https://doi.org/10.1016/j.cub.2016.02.063.

Tamisiea, Jack. "Genes Reveal How Some Rockfish Live up to 200 Years." *Scientific American*, November 11, 2021. https://www.scientificamerican.com/article/genes-reveal-how-some-rockfish-live-up-to-200-years.

Turner, John. "The Slave Graves." Saint Helena Island Info. Accessed August 4, 2022. http://sainthelenaisland.info/slavegraves.htm.

United States Census Bureau. "U.S. and World Population Clock." Accessed February 12, 2022. https://www.census.gov/popclock.

United States Environmental Protection Agency. "Mosquito Life Cycle." Accessed October 1, 2022. https://www.epa.gov/mosquitocontrol/mosquito-life-cycle.

Van der Linden, Sander. "The Science Behind Dreaming." *Scientific American*, July 26, 2011. https://www.scientificamerican.com/article/the-science-behind-dreaming.

Völter, Christoph J., Roger Mundry, Josep Call, and Amanda Seed. "Chimpanzees Flexibly Update Working Memory Contents and Show Susceptibility to Distraction in the Self-Ordered Search Task." *Proceedings of the Royal Society B* 286, no. 1907 (2019): 20190715. https://doi.org/10.1098/rspb.2019.0715.

Wahlberg, Magnus, and Hakan Westerberg. "Sounds Produced by Herring (*Clupea harengus*) Bubble Release." *Aquatic Living Resources* 16, no. 3 (2003): 271–275. https://doi.org/10.1016/S0990-7440(03)00017-2.

Wanjek, Christopher. "Sleep Shrinks the Brain—and That's a Good Thing." *Scientific American*, February 3, 2017. https://www.scientificamerican.com/article/sleep-shrinks-the-brain-and-thats-a-good-thing/#:~:text=The%2520researchers%2520found%2520that%2520sleep,new%2520things,%2520the%2520researchers%2520said.

Washington Department of Fish and Wildlife. "Rougheye Rockfish." Accessed September 3, 2022. https://wdfw.wa.gov/species-habitats/species/sebastes-aleutianus.

Welsh, Tim. "It Feels Instantaneous, But How Long Does It Really Take to Think a Thought?" *The Conversation*, June 26, 2015. https://theconversation.com/it-feels-instantaneous-but-how-long-does-it-really-take-to-think-a-thought-42392.

Williamson, A. M., and Anne-Marie Feyer. "Moderate Sleep Deprivation Produces Impairments in Cognitive and Motor Performance Equivalent to Legally Prescribed Levels of Alcohol Intoxication." Occupational and Environmental Medicine 57, 10. (2000): 649–655. https://doi.org/10.1136/oem.57.10.649

Wilson, Ben, Robert S. Batty, and Lawrence M. Dill. "Pacific and Atlantic Herring Produce Burst Pulse Sounds." *Proceedings of the Royal Society B* 271, Suppl_3 (2004). https://doi.org/10.1098/rsbl.2003.0107.

World Health Organization. "The Global Health Observatory." Accessed October 13, 2022. https://www.who.int/data/gho/data/themes/mortality-and-global-health-estimates/ghe-life-expectancy-and-healthy-life-expectancy.

Xie, Lulu, et al. "Sleep Drives Metabolite Clearance from the Adult Brain." *Science* 342, no. 6156 (2013): 373–377. https://doi.org/10.1126/science.1241224.

Yamazaki, Risa, H. Toda, P. Libourel, Y. Hayashi, K. Vogt, and T. Sakurai. "Evolutionary Origin of Distinct NREM and REM Sleep." *Frontiers in Psychology* 11 (2019). https://doi.org/10.3389/fpsyg.2020.567618.

Yassa, Michael A. "Hippocampus." *Encyclopaedia Britannica Online.* Accessed March 5, 2022. https://www.britannica.com/science/hippocampus.

Zanette, Liana Y., Emma C. Hobbs, Lauren E. Witterick, Scott A. MacDougall-Shackleton, and Michael Clinchy. "Predator-Induced Fear Causes PTSD-Like Changes in the Brains and Behaviour of Wild Animals." *Scientific Reports* 9 (2019): 11474. https://doi.org/10.1038/s41598-019-47684-6.

Zimmer, Carl. "100 Trillion Connections: New Efforts Probe and Map the Brain's Detailed Architecture." *Scientific American*, January 1, 2011. https://www.scientificamerican.com/article/100-trillion-connections.

ACKNOWLEDGMENTS

Special thanks to the researchers, animal care providers, and other experts who contributed their time and resources to this book.

Innovative Octopuses

Dr. Anahí Espíndola, evolutionary ecologist at the University of Maryland in College Park • Zoë Hagberg, aquarist at the Shedd Aquarium • Ruby Ibarra, rapper, poet, and scientist • Dr. Jennifer Mather, octopus cognition researcher at the University of Lethbridge • Dr. Elizabeth Sibert, biological oceanographer at Yale University • Dr. Dominic Sivitilli, astrobiologist

Panic-Busting Parrots

Dr. Lorin Lindner, clinical psychologist and founder of Lockwood Animal Rescue Center and Serenity Park Sanctuary • Kerry Netherton, recreation supervisor at the Czorny Alzheimer Centre • Stan McDonald, foreman of Lockwood Animal Rescue Center/Serenity Park Sanctuary • Dr. Antonia Seligowski, neuroscientist and clinical psychologist at McLean Hospital and Harvard Medical School • Dr. Liana Zanette, conservation, population, and behavioral ecologist at Western University

Savvy Squirrels

Paula Holman, WildCare squirrel foster care volunteer • Dr. Robert Full, professor and director Poly-PEDAL Laboratory at the University of California, Berkeley • Dr. Lucia Jacobs, professor of psychology and neuroscience and director of the Jacobs Laboratory of Cognitive Biology at the University of California, Berkeley • Dr. Daniel Koditschek, Alfred Fitler Moore Professor of Electrical and Systems Engineering and member of Penn's General Robotics, Automation, Sensing & Perception (GRASP) Lab • Melanie Piazza, director of Animal Care and Hospital Operations at WildCare • Dr. Gina Poe, Eleanor Leslie Chair in Innovative Brain Research and director of the Poe Lab at the University of California, Los Angeles

Half-Brained Birds

Bret Nainoa Mossman, biologist at the Hawai'i Island Natural Area Reserve System • Dr. Ravi Nath, geneticist at Stanford University • Dr. Gina Poe, Eleanor Leslie Chair in Innovative Brain Research and director of the Poe Lab at the University of California, Los Angeles • Dr. Niels Rattenborg, sleep scientist and research leader of the Avian Sleep Group at the Max Planck Institute for Biological Intelligence

Timeless Tortoises

Dr. Steve Austad, distinguished professor and co-director of the University of Alabama at Birmingham Nathan Shock Center of Excellence in the Basic Biology of Aging, senior scientific director at the American Federation for Aging Research • Dr. Kevin Coffey, post-doctoral scholar at the University of Washington School of Medicine • Dr. Joe Hollins, veterinarian surgeon • Dr. Gretchen Johnson, biologist • Dr. Maria Pia Miglietta, associate professor at Texas A&M University at Galveston • Dr. Richard A. Miller, director of the Paul F. Glenn Center for Biology of Aging Research at the University of Michigan

Chatty Cetaceans

Dr. Jacob Andreas, assistant professor of Electrical Engineering and Computer Science at the Massachusetts Institute of Technology (MIT) and on the machine learning team at Project CETI • Dr. Rodrigo Braga, assistant professor of Neurology and director of the Human Cognitive Neuroscience Lab at Northwestern University • Dr. Michelle Fournet, director of the Sound Science Research Collective • Dr. Shane Gero, founder of the Dominica Sperm Whale Project and scientist-in-residence at Carleton University • Dr. David Gruber, distinguished professor at City University of New York and project lead for Project CETI

Other Material

Dr. Eric H. Chudler, neuroscientist and executive director of the Center for Neurotechnology at the University of Washington • Cara Giaimo, science writer

A special thanks to Amy Brand and Bill Smith at MIT Press, to Karen Lotz at Candlewick Press, and to the wonderful editorial and design team who made this book possible, especially Hilary Van Dusen, Mona Baloch, and Rachel Wood. Additional thanks to Seth Mnookin; Drs. Sarah, Rachel, and Laura Schwartz; Dr. Alan Lightman; and to my family.

IMAGE CREDITS

INDEX

CHRISTINA COUCH is the coauthor, with Cara Giaimo, of *Detector Dogs, Dynamite Dolphins, and More Animals with Super Sensory Powers*. She is an alumna of the MIT Graduate Program in Science Writing, and when she isn't writing books, she writes about brains and lots of other weird science for *NOVA*, the *New York Times*, *Wired*, and other outlets.

DANIEL DUNCAN is the illustrator of the first Extraordinary Animals book, *Detector Dogs, Dynamite Dolphins, and More Animals with Super Sensory Powers*, and of *Mr. Posey's New Glasses* by Ted Kooser, *The Girl Who Could Fix Anything* by Mara Rockliff, and *The Purple Puffy Coat* by Maribeth Boelts. Daniel Duncan creates most of his work in an old stable turned studio on the outskirts of London.